TIM BRAGG

LYRICS TO LIVE BY

Keys to Self-Help

Notes for a Better Life

Ian Wilson - Photography

About the author

Tim Bragg is a novelist, short-story writer, an occasional writer of nonsense verse and poetry and from time to time writes articles on various topics. He is also a musician and singer-songwriter. Tim plays various instruments, including, drums, flute and guitar. He has recorded several CD albums.

Tim studied English and American Literature at Warwick University. Married to a French woman, Tim currently lives in France. They have one son.

Tim has always been interested in the way folk think and act: why we behave the way we do and how we can improve our lives.

Contents

"Slip slidin' away Slip slidin' away You know the nearer your destination The more you're slip slidin' away."

- 'Slip Slidin' Away' - Paul Simon

"You can't always get what you want/ but if you try sometimes well, you might find/ you get what you need."

-'You Can't Always Get What You Want' – Jagger/Richards

"Anytime you feel the pain, hey Jude, refrain/Don't carry the world upon your shoulders."

-'Hey Jude' – Paul McCartney (credited: Lennon-McCartney)

"There's still time to change the road you're on."

-'Stairway to Heaven' – Page/Plant

"All the money you made/Will never buy back your soul."

-'Masters of War' - Bob Dylan

"In the burning heart/ Just about to burst/ There's a quest for answers/ An unquenchable thirst."

- 'Burning Heart' - Jim Peterik / Frank Sullivan

"What a wicked game you played to make me feel this way/ What a wicked thing to do to let me dream of you/ What a wicked thing to say you never felt this way/ What a wicked thing to do to make me dream of you."

-'Wicked Game' - Chris Isaak

"Don't it always seem to go/ That you don't know what you've got till it's gone."

- 'Big Yellow Taxi' – Joni Mitchell

"I smile when I'm angry/ I cheat and I lie/ I do what I have to do/ To get by."

-'In my secret life' - Leonard Cohen/Sharon Robinson

"Love is careless in its choosing/ Sweeping over cross a baby/ Love descends on those defenceless/ Idiot love will spark the fusion

Inspirations have I none/ Just to touch the flaming dove/ All I have is my love of love/ And love is not loving."

-'Soul Love' - David Bowie

"In the morning/ I'm at work on time/ My boss, he tells me/ That I'm doing fine/ When I'm going home/ Whiskey bottle Movie on TV/ Memories make me cry

- 'Questioningly' - Ramones

"And I can feel the stars getting closer/ And I can feel you by my side/ And I can feel an arm wrap around me/ Yes I can feel you by my side/ Don't look back 'cus it's coming/ Don't look here 'cus it's gone/ And when you least expect it will fall upon your shoulder/ Sometimes stand still – better not run."

- 'Some Answers' - Tim Bragg

Foreword

It has been a great pleasure to write *Lyrics to Live by* and I think – in its writing – I have also been guided and helped.

Firstly, I must stress, that I have treated these fragments of lyrics solely on their own merits. They have not been contextualised. I deliberately didn't read the whole of the song's lyrics, even if I knew the songs themselves. The idea was to take a phrase, an interesting sample, and ruminate on that. Often, we are drawn to a lyric in a song. We might well sing along to a refrain (a repeated chorus) but some lyrics stick out and call to us siren-like. In fact, we can be drawn to certain lyrics at certain times in our lives and – indeed – interpret these lyrics differently at different times in our lives.

All these lyrics were given to me by the publisher except for Paul Simon's *Slip Slidin' Away* and my own contribution *Some Answers* (which I felt relevant to include). My approach was to read and think about the lyrics – but not to over-think them. Then I would begin writing – almost as if meditating. By focusing my mind on the lyrics' meaning, I achieved some mental clarity – maintaining contemplation as I wrote. Thus, the act of writing was near automatic and self-beneficial. Without sounding too fey – this process of writing helped me see things in the words I perhaps hadn't expected. This mix of contemplation and automatic-writing (as if I opened a channel to a higher consciousness) certainly helped me; as I hope it will help you.

Of course, poetry has been a means to help and develop and cultivate the human experience for thousands of years (think of Homer's oral epics: 'The Iliad' and 'The Odyssey') and poetry has innate rhythm of course. But when we hear lyrics they are inseparable from the music, there is a strange symbiosis whereby the lyrics are infused by the music (and given extra effect) and the lyrics give 'meaning' to the music. The abstraction of music is given greater accessibility and focus by the words within. Music tells stories. And when the music ends – passing through time - it can only be reanimated by being re-played. But the lyrics can be read at any time. (Music can of course be written down but there are few who can look at a score and hear the melody and harmony, let alone if reading for multi-instrumentation. Playing music makes it live – over and over and over.)

Yet lyrics mostly do not convert to stand-alone poetry (and vice versa). When we read a lyric, it is imbued by the song's legacy and – again – brought to life through its melody. Lyrics often speak to us in a 'folk tongue' and here I don't mean folk music (although folk music is not excluded) but rather the experiences, thoughts, ideas of 'ordinary' folk translating those inner experiences through words applied to music. I have to say here too, that when I write songs the words come to me at the same time as the music (though they might get altered slightly afterwards) but that symbiosis is seemingly intrinsic. I know others work differently and there are many examples of writing partners where one takes care of the music and the other the words. But many do find words and harmony/melody arriving together.

For decades - and of course way back in time through Victorian parlours with friends/families gathered round a piano to wandering minstrels or work-songs or lullabies - lyrics have saturated our daily experience. Songs are everywhere. But we are drawn to songs and musicians who seem to speak directly to us. They become part of us. They really do help guide us through life and come to our aid when most needed. At our lowest, a song can be played over and over, and this repetition seems to heal. When we are blue a blues song seems to do the trick. And the very personal nature of a song makes it effective for our own personal situation – bad/good or otherwise. I am thankful to the musicians who wrote songs that helped me through difficult times: the end of a love affair, for instance.

So here we have a collection of quite disparate songs and their lyrics. From the '60s through the following decades and including some heavy-weight writers (Lennon-McCartney/Bowie/Dylan) and – naturally – various styles of music. The lyrics are very different in tone, but each has its nugget of wisdom to be mined.

What are my qualifications for writing this book? Well, I am a musician and I write songs (and I write novels/short-stories too). I also have a degree in English and American literature and I tend to think about things a lot! Thus, I can only hope that my interpretation of the lyrics is helpful to you and/or resonates in some way. If only in that you re-evaluate the role of lyrics in songs, after all it's easy just to let things wash over you. My attempt here has been to stop and shine a light directly on the words. Let's check these words out. What are they saying? How can they help us? How can we draw strength and hope through them? Why not!? As said, lyrics are part of us. They can help guide us through this life. They are accessible, songs truly can be 'guides'.

Two of the lyricists I most admire: Phil Lynott and Van Morrison are not in this collection. But if this book resonates and I am called upon to do another then you can be sure they will be included. They have certainly helped me through my life's journey. (Van Morrison indirectly led me to study English at university.) You will all have your favourites. Here, all I can trust, is that I have given you a key, a way, to think about those lyrics - perhaps in a deeper fashion. Or for you to understand the power of lyrics throughout your life. Perhaps for you to listen and look at those lyrics you love anew.

And with that I truly hope this book will be of some service. *'You might* [just] *find you get what you need'*!

Chapter 1

"Slip slidin' away
Slip slidin' away
You know the nearer your destination
The more you're slip slidin' away."

- 'Slip Slidin' Away' - Paul Simon

Artist: Paul Simon. Album: *Greatest Hits, Etc.* Year: 1977

These lyrics really sing to me! They resonate inside my head like any good melody and lyric should. There's something deeply melancholic about them and a feeling, perhaps, of a courageous struggle.

The first thing to observe is the idea of a 'destination'. Doesn't this idea plague our lives? It would be called 'goal orientated'. There is something within us that wants, even needs, to achieve, arrive, aim for, aim at. Beyond this there is the greater idea that we are going somewhere, going someplace. Is our ultimate destination – death?

Then there is the idea that no matter how hard you try, the destination you have set upon, cannot be reached. It is elusive. It's easy to have the image of a green grassed hill, you want to get to its summit. But close to your goal the grass has worn away and become mud. You slip, and you slide, and you fall back. And there is even the idea that this is a constant struggle – that there is no end to your slippin' and slidin'. Of course, here I am reminded of King Sisyphus and his interminable task of rolling a boulder up a steep hill. Zeus - the punisher of his trickery – used trickery himself and thus each time the boulder was close to the summit it rolled back down again to the foot of the hill. (Sisyphus had cheated Thanatos, Death, by tricking him into showing how his chains worked – and seizing the opportunity to chain Thanatos himself! For a while there was no death upon the earth.)

As a child – perhaps not knowing the story behind the Sisyphean struggle – I always felt sorry for Sisyphus and his eternal labour. He paid dearly for his hubris and deceit. But as ever, to me, it seemed the gods had gone too far. If you read his story, you'll hear more of his duplicity. Here I am also reminded of Camus' idea that Sisyphus represented the absurdity of human life but that he would have been 'happy' in this eternal struggle.

It's rather like the Russian 'worker' in the USSR (Union of Soviet Socialist Republics) who was an exceptionally hard-working and zealous person who gave the name to Stakhanovite struggle. (Solzhenitsyn displays this zealous hard work in *One Day in the Life of Ivan Denisovitch*.)

Is life a meaningless round of repetitive struggle that never reaches its goals? Are we all engaged in Sisyphean struggle?

Maybe Paul Simon's lyrics are poking us – teasing us - are cynical. Maybe they're reflective. Defeatist. Maybe not!

We all have our goals and we all face our ultimate destination. We all fail. And we all give ourselves a very hard time for this failure. Even the destination of death is viewed in terms of a failure to be 'the best we could' 'a good/great person' 'a moral person'. The idea that we will be judged by our actions (as Sisyphus was) is intrinsic to our culture. But let's view this in a different manner.

Firstly – let's look at this life we have and lead as best we can. In many ways life IS a struggle and there is no denying this. We keep climbing that hill. The burden can be heavy. We all know and understand this. We set ourselves goals and so often fail to reach them OR fail to appreciate we have reached them. Many times, we HAVE reached them only to see the next hill as the goal. That hill we DID climb – O that was nothing, this next hill, this MOUNTAIN that needs to be scaled and the summit reached, that's far more important. If I don't reach that summit I am a failure! But did you enjoy the climb – the struggle, each step you took? The view close to the summit is near to the view from the summit. And why this need to continue to climb an ever-increasing number of summits? Is this Human Nature?

If parts of us are focussed on setting goals and standards and struggling towards them is it – in fact – in Human Nature, ever to be satisfied? Perhaps it is the struggle which is important. I imagine most of you have at some point climbed a hill. The further you go up the harder it is to climb, but the final step to the summit is wonderful. You pant, you double-over in exhaustion but you are exhilarated. The view is great. You feel 'on top of the world'. There is a sense of achievement. And then you gaze at the next summit. Do you carry on; do you sit down and enjoy where you are; do you set off down the hill straight away? Do you reflect on each of your steps and the breaths you have taken? Once a hill is climbed there are thousands more, once a mountain is climbed there are a thousand more. Can you distinguish the euphoria of being on the summit from that first step you took from base camp? You can't separate the goal from the process and even if you FAIL to reach the summit that does NOT negate the effort and determination to try.

As a musician I often think about my struggle to be better; that is a huge subject. Mozart was perhaps the most accomplished composer we have known. Was he perfect? Had he reached the summit of perfection? Of course, not – though his music is so often sublime. Some musicians, some composers are 'better' than others – appreciated more than others, some might remain undiscovered. But all true musicians are forcing themselves up the steepness of their craft, their technique, their expression, their search for that elusive 'something special'. It is the acceptance that one is going to slip and slide away from that summit that maintains the struggle and effort. Do we give up? Do we slide down to the bottom and stay there?

For every one of our failures or perceived failures we have a choice in the manner we respond. For instance, throughout my time as a musician I have had goals (even if they weren't 'set' they were in my mind). Looking back, I can see how easily these achievements have been brushed aside as I set out on yet another mountain to climb. Sometimes I am reminded to look back (from my current climb?) and acknowledge my journey from its beginning (having no skills whatsoever) to where I am now. And I must say at this point that it is SO easy to judge yourself against others, how they all seem to be scaling Mount Everest. I really believe that all those others – doing so much better than we are – are thinking the same. If you are true to yourself then the journey is never done.

Every goal we set and that we strive for will bring something into our lives: wisdom/vigour/renewed hope/learnt skills/optimism/courage/confidence – the list goes on. THAT is what we need to concentrate and reflect on. Every time we set out on whichever quest we set - we will be changed in some fashion. We may or may not reach our destination, but we will learn so much about ourselves as we struggle towards that summit. Enjoy it! Enjoy it for what it is – the goal orientation is helpful at directing our efforts, but it really isn't the 'be all and end all'. Ask yourself – in all your endeavours – how you have changed from their beginning to their end – or from their beginning through the continued effort to where you are now. If you slipped or if you slid – how has that helped and/or changed you? Is anything worth its attainment if it comes too easily? If you walk along a plateau to get to your goal – how would your sense of accomplishment feel?

And now I want to talk of that end destination, the end of life (at least as we know and understand it on this earth). We think of this as our 'final destination', maybe it is and maybe it isn't. Some of us will get pulled there despite our feet slippin' and slidin' in resistance. Some may just lie back on the side of the hill and be pulled to the summit. Here as we get 'nearer our destination' we might feel we're 'slip slidin' away' but this summit is inevitable. I think through our lives – and at different times we view our place in the world (and the world itself) very differently - we need to appraise all our struggles, all our missed opportunities, all our near summit ascents, all our continued efforts to be better than what we were. NONE of this is to be negated. **Everything you have striven for has made you who you are.** To slip and slide is to be truly human. To continue to climb towards the summit is the best of being human. We do that for its own reward. We certainly CAN accept our place in the world and be reasonable in our assessment of ourselves but also give ourselves some praise for trying. For not giving up. For becoming better people against all the odds.

At the end of our life we will leave our legacy. What will folk remember of us? That we had a smart, new car and x thousand in the bank – or how we behaved in life? Do you recall Eddie the Eagle? He entered the 1988

Olympic ski jumping competition and competed at 70 and 90 meters. He was the sole British entrant and the only one to represent Great Britain in this event since 1928. He was an amateur, but he was determined (in 1990 the rules were changed so that someone such as Eddie wouldn't be able to perform). He epitomised the British 'underdog' spirit. Here really was someone slippin' and slidin' from their destination. And yet – despite his failure – he came last in both distances – he has become someone to admire. In fact, he has had many opportunities in life as a 'failed sportsman' and has become something of a celebrity. Was his heroic attempt to compete at this level pointless? Will he be judged negatively against those who had all the facilities and experience to WIN medals? Should there be a judgement at death – would his courage and determination trump any gold, silver or bronze medal? What is TRULY important in this life?

We must of course try and measure ourselves against ourselves and no other. We will also be judged on ourselves and no other, I believe. You try, you don't succeed (as you had wished), you try again. This is the noble spirit of humanity. Easy fame, easy fortune, even an easy accomplished and 'good' character are nothing compared with those who have had to work so very hard to be who they are. At the final summit – the end of our life – we will have embodied every moment we have ever experienced. We will have become the sum of this experience. Were we to be given the grace at death to look back (and there is much evidence to suggest there is at least the possibility of a past-life review) then – and only then – can we know our true effect upon the earth, upon others and upon ourselves.

Don't give up. Whatever you are striving for or towards – don't give up. And here I am reminded of the beautifully sung and emotionally charged Perter Gabriel song *Don't Give Up* where he and Kate Bush urge us to carry on despite all.

Are we crafted through adversity? We certainly must carry that weight, but if we must carry our own burden then let's carry a good weight – unlike Sisyphus who was being punished – we can take up our challenges in good heart and spirit, this life is not infinite and there may be sweeter fields and meadows beyond. Maybe some hills and mountains too.

You may slip – you may slide. You may not reach your destination – BUT – you will be a finer human being in each attempt you make. Keep your eyes looking up, keep strong and courageous. Even if you slip and slide – keep your feet on the ground. Keep trying. Be patient. And remember you are not alone.

Chapter 2

"You can't always get what you want/but if you try sometimes well, you might find/ you get what you need."

- 'You Can't Always Get What You Want' – Jagger/Richards

Artist: Rolling Stones. Album: *Let it Bleed* Year: 1969

If you try sometimes – you might get what you need, not what you want. But what does this lyric really say and how should we relate to it? Perhaps if it had said: if you 'don't try' sometimes you might, at least, get what you need - would that have made more sense? Is it saying – try and achieve what you want and 'in the process' you might not get what you have been struggling for, but in fact and at least, get what you need?

None of us can always get what we want. And that's a good thing! If you had always got what you wanted that might well have worked against you developing as a balanced, good or better human being. As a child we are full of wants – but our parents or guardians act as modifiers to these wants (we would hope and presume). What is the value of our 'wants'? What is beguiling us; where does the notion of what is worth valuing (wanted) come from? Is it intrinsic or extrinsic? Who gives us these values: our parents, the Media, our surrounding culture, our religions, ourselves?

If we fall short in getting what (we think) we want, then many times 'having what we need' becomes the better option! What is the relationship between what is wanted and what is needed? Who decides that? Is it a matter of accepting second-best? Or is it, rather, in the acknowledgement that in fact what we 'need' is REALLY what we want! We have been hoodwinked by our desires. In not obtaining our desires we get what is better for us – what is right for us.

Can't having what we want be right for us too?

Where do these wants come from - who dictates them? Why are we so compelled by needs and desires? In looking for the wood do we miss all those beautiful surrounding trees? It's almost as if we punish ourselves for the desires of our desires! And having what is right for us – what we NEED - is not a failing. It's wisdom. And is part of our wanting something, simply measuring ourselves against others? You want a luxury car, a handsome husband, a job that pays extremely well. Nothing wrong with these wants *per se*. But WHY do you want them? What is driving your desires?

We are not always clear with ourselves about our wants and desires. These wants are planted within us and we feel inadequate, less, lacking, if we don't get them. We want a luxury car – top end of the market, fast, comfortable and above-all expensive! Of course, we can say that having a well-made car that looks great IS a good thing. If we have the money and can afford it, why not? If we can't afford it then the safe, reliable, family saloon becomes our only option (again depending on money). I know The Rolling Stone's lyric also talks about love (not just material desires) and I will talk about that too – but let's keep concentrated on this materialistic aspect. Whichever car you buy you'll probably have been affected by the car manufacturer's marketing. Or by the advice and/or experience of a friend, or your bank balance etc.

Let's presume you have bought your heart's-desire XXXX (make and model of relevant car). Your neighbours are impressed (and jealous). You feel quite smug. But someone 'keys' the side of your shiny new car when you've parked in town. You drive too fast. You get a speeding ticket. You feel confident and superior when driving about - self-important. You get challenged to some races – but you decline. You wash the car twice a week. No matter how clean - the value of the car depreciates rapidly. Your wife/husband tells you that you think more about that car than them! Well, let's not kid ourselves, the driving experience and handling of the car is superb, and it certainly cost a packet. But after a year, everyone KNOWS the make of the car on your drive and don't much care. The insurance renewal is sky-high. You won't let your child drive the car for fear of them going too fast and crashing. The initial wonderment has become routine. It is JUST a car after-all. Though a very expensive and well-made one. And you deserved it, didn't you? Didn't you!

Now let's switch the scenario. You buy a YYYY (make and relevant model), it's comfortable enough and it drives fast enough for the road conditions with a little extra when lateness requires some speed. No-one is particularly impressed, the insurance is low and you're happy for your child to drive it. It runs well and has a high MPG (miles per gallon), you don't worship it and yet you value its service. It is a tool. It helps you get from A to Z.

Now you didn't get what you wanted but rather what seemed 'second-best'. You DID save a lot of money getting YYYY.

A few months later someone very dear to you is taken ill and they need you to stay with them and help financially (as they've lost their job due to their ill-health). You can afford to take some time off and stay with them – and this because you bought the car you needed NOT the car you had set your heart on. Life threw out what seemed like a forced disappointment, but you got what you needed and THEN later there came a pay-off you couldn't possibly have foreseen. Fanciful? Pragmatic?

But you DESERVED the stylish, smart, expensive car, didn't you? That was your reward for hard work. Work you didn't necessarily enjoy. It wasn't so much a luxury, but rather, well a present. Your status would have been emphasised by such a gift to yourself. It would have been a badge to the world – a symbol of who you are and what you've achieved. A tangible representation of you and your status.

While looking after your ill friend you get back a sense of what exactly it is that you deserve and need in your life. Their gratitude and love for your unselfish behaviour, support and care is exactly what you NEED. And though they may have wanted full health (which was unavailable to them) they got what they needed - in YOU. These ideas take time to sink into your brain, everything seems unfair. Then news footage such as children being bombed to pieces somewhere in the world acts as a catalyst to different thoughts. Your friend is much better and arrives at your family home. Long talks with them emphasise what THEY deem as important. They needed to be better to live, wanting life is not a luxury. And getting what they needed brought them what they wanted.

You then begin to distil this idea of want/need throughout your life. I mean it seemed like you never got what you wanted, and yet, contrast this with wanting more, and getting more and then wanting more, it never stops, and it drives you crazy – I want I want. You get. I want I want. You get. Why would this hunger, this thirst be satiated or quenched? It can't be.

How many of us who have found love in our life have done so on a trail of previous: 'she's the one' or 'he's the love of my life'. In fact, a series of unrequited loves or failures, At the time we are besotted and crave this 'someone'. We CRAVE this other to give us what we think we need. Yes, they are most certainly THE ONE. No doubt about it. We want and want and want till it hurts. But if it doesn't work out or never happens we feel that our 'want' has been betrayed. Yet from the standpoint of hindsight (if happy in a relationship - or perhaps even if not!) we can say – thank God that DIDN'T work out! **We feel saved.**

The persons we thought we needed are incomparable with the ones we now have – or perhaps in living a solitary life we understand that that is better for us than living with a person who is wrong and/or damaging for us. What's that saying: Rejection is God's protection. Could easily be: Rejection is OUR life's protection. It really isn't always good to get what we want. Because when we want we are susceptible. We must trust in life's needs, not in our selfish desires. As Ian Anderson wrote (Jethro Tull): *Life's a long song.* And: *if you wait then your plate I will fill.*

They put chocolates at the sides of tills because as we pay for our food (our needs) we are tempted to add something sweet as a treat. We are constantly manipulated by life. We are constantly manipulated by advertising and The Media. How can and do we guard against this? Well, we can use empirical evidence from our lives to discern what is needed from what is wanted. We (should) learn from the past. But in love – at least – discernment and logic can easily fly out of the window. Are we able to analyse ourselves constantly or at regular intervals? Well we CAN know ourselves. That takes time too. Maybe we should just ACCEPT ourselves and our wants and needs? Who cares, eh?

Wants and Needs are irrevocably intertwined are they not? There's a kind of symbiosis, wants feed from our perceived needs. Needs seem to feed on the desire of our wants. We can feel like puppets at times. Helpless to our desires. Played by our desires. The Buddhist might say – do away with desire for peace and contentment. And they may well be right. But for most of us we dance to whichever tune is played the loudest.

There is no true happiness to be found in constant desire. Constant want. There can't be and our lives progress in a manner that surely makes that self-evident. Some quiet reflection and wisdom is necessary to see that. We must stop comparing ourselves to others too. Stop comparing with those better off and those worse off. It isn't fair on either of them – especially those that are worse off. And I always wonder is there someone who has NO-ONE who is worse off? This all feeds either the green-eyed monster or our fragile ego.

An artist might constantly compare their art with others, their peers, or those they can aspire to or those they can compare their progress with. But it doesn't really affect anything other than their perception of themselves. You can use those 'below' to measure your growth or those 'above' to measure how far you must travel, but for the actual relationship between the artists and their music – nothing changes. It is what it is. If you want to be a better artist, then learn the skills, the techniques (painting, music, acting, sculpting, writing etc.). And you will need to have certain proficiencies for different stages of your growth/development. Be yourself. Be as good as you can be.

A musician can survive with less knowledge/technique playing pop or blues in a pub gig than playing, say, classical music in a professional orchestra. The satisfaction though might well be the same. What does the musician need compared to what is wanted? But wanting something in this context is to set foot on the pathway to all the various needs that will eventually be required. **If you want to improve you will need to do certain things.** These are not empty, or distracting wants. Wanting to be a 'star' on the other hand is...

You can't always get what you want. But sometimes you CAN. It's not always about sufficiency. Sometimes you do get that girl/boy you had longed for at a distance. You do get bought that silver flute - and then find that your needs in flute playing are more easily met. Occasionally you might get a 'want' that takes time to realise, something long held but hidden and imprisoned through fear and time. You might find you get what you need – or, I guess, you might not. There are some basic needs in this life: food, shelter, protection, love (from a parent or spouse or child or friend). Maybe a sense of who we are and some related worth. Maslow developed a pyramid of needs – check it out. My list contains the very basics. Lots of humans get by on the basics but they are no less complex in their desires and needs.

I wonder what Mick Jagger wants in his life – or Keith Richards? Do they need anything else? A longer life? To be younger perhaps? Surely no more hit records are needed. Perhaps to make a difference to someone out there, or someone close. Maybe to understand who they are and where they fit into this world and its seven billion human inhabitants. Could those, as then, young men ever have imagined the impact of their music and lyrics?

Wants can grow, wants are self-perpetuating, eating themselves and growing forever fatter. Look around you. What is it you want in your life – really, and what is it you need in your life – really. All the decisions about wants/needs are yours. You may not have control over outside influences and opportunities – but you have got control over yourself.

Chapter 3

"Anytime you feel the pain, hey Jude, refrain/Don't carry the world upon your shoulders."

- 'Hey Jude' – Paul McCartney (credited: Lennon-McCartney).

Artist: The Beatles (*single release*). Year: 1968

Don't carry the world upon your shoulders, I mean who would? Much too heavy. Any way we can't possibly; can we? Can we?

Carrying the world upon your shoulders; from the worries and concerns of the world in general, to the worries and concerns of ourselves, our lives, our families, our friends. The MACRO and the MICRO.

The MACRO

What's the point of shouldering the concerns of the world? Refrain! Don't do it!

But haven't we the moral duty to do so? Is it not imperative as human beings to worry and be concerned and thus take on the burden of others? Not just others but the whole of Nature – its flora and fauna. Is that a moral imperative? If we don't who will. Look how we care – look how we suffer. Look how hard we make it on ourselves and thus show solidarity with everyone and everything's suffering.

Question: If you suffer do you want others to suffer along with you? You might want them to be concerned, but surely not to carry YOUR burden. Only you can do that can't you? And if others suffer as you suffer then that only magnifies the suffering and does nothing to alleviate it!

If you wouldn't want others to suffer for you – why do you suffer for others? Why try and carry a weight that is too heavy? Why give yourself a hernia or muscle strain trying to pick something up you can't? It's nonsensical isn't it?

That's not to say you can't DO things. That's not to say you can't make a difference. That's not to say that you shouldn't feel sympathy or empathy. It's about choosing the weight you can take from the world – which might be a very small weight, and you know that if we ALL took a few ounces or grammes then we could ALL make a difference.

You feel wearied by your load. Look at the world – look at the way it is. The war, the hunger, the poverty, the starving, the cruelty, the destruction, the destruction of us and our fellow animals and the nature we all live in. But what can we do?

You can't alleviate war by going to war – violence begets violence, have we never and will we never learn? You can watch the world go to war but not take up arms, or you can enlist and fight. If you choose to observe and are crushed by the horror and violence - you will indeed be MENTALLY crushed by this horror and violence. Your mood will darken, and you might feel exonerated by your state of morality. You will maintain this 'morality' as you watch children blown to pieces. Okay I'm being a little hard on you. But being passively burdened by information does you or others no good. Being in a dark mood does neither you nor others any good. But you can't help it? You can't help yourself? Stop. Think. Analyse.

STOP – if your actions add nothing to the situation then there is no point taking on an imaginary load.

THINK – what, in fact, COULD you do (or not do) to help.

ANALYSE – think about those ideas and how you might be able to do them or refrain from doing them. What power have you? The power to give yourself, your time, your energy, your money. To hold yourself back, to wait, to withhold energy AND money. (Or divert all these things.)

SPECIFICALLY – WAR. You can fight, help make arms and ammunition, give medical help, raise money. You can refuse to fight (or not volunteer to fight) – protest, channel money into anti-war activity. You can ignore the war completely (unless or until it touches you).

Here I am reminded of the film 'Shenandoah' and how the patriarch of the family – despite all his efforts, becomes involved in the Civil War – yet struggles to keep his children out of the fighting. Eventually the war 'touches him', and his sons go to fight. His youngest son is mistaken for a soldier and captured. Another is killed. The patriarch is played by James Stewart who flew air missions over Germany in World War Two. In 'Shenandoah' the family and the nation - or nations depending on your point of view - are effectively destroyed – at least the Confederate States.

It all comes down to a flow of moral decisions. That is what we are as humans. We make constant decisions. But. And this is the point to be made - a decision only means something if it has any impact and if that impact doesn't outweigh one's own mental and physical stability. Certainly, sometimes decisions are made whereby people sacrifice themselves for others. This is certainly taking on the burden of others – but is a noble thing. Not everyone can do this. We say there are brave people and cowards – but I wonder if there are 'just' (simply) decisions made in the moment.

If you can do nothing about a foreign war you believe unjust other than to protest or speak your mind. Do that. If others don't listen – there's nothing you can do about that. Don't make yourself ill. Don't feel so frustrated. Don't let anger turn in on yourself. As soon as you do that you are again carrying the burden that is too heavy for you.

Imagine a friend of yours seems bent under the weight of their worries – you would probably do two things.

1. Take any of the weight you can manage from them. (Give them a lift somewhere to sort out a problem... lend or give them some money to tide them over.)

2. Talk to them and be with them and explain lovingly that the weight they are carrying is an imposed burden that does neither them nor the weight any good. The weight doesn't NEED to be carried. Some weight – the good stuff – doesn't even weigh anything! *'He ain't heavy he's my brother'*! You'd get them to understand the futility of their carrying of the burden. So – if you'd do this for a loved one why do you/would you allow yourself to be so burdened?

THE MICRO

Here two guilts like rushing rivers stream into one another. Not only is there the guilt of feeling inadequate (the MACRO - being unable to affect events in the world) but the guilt of feeling unable to alter oneself (the MICRO). Carrying the weight of being oneself. The two can be linked.

We take pride in being good people, thoughtful people. We improve ourselves by 'looking in' - reflecting upon our actions and thoughts. But then we allow ourselves such sensitivity when reacting with the outside world and its effects. We analyse and examine our motives (and this involves our relationship with others and the world in general with all its affairs) and our responses and actions. By becoming better, we run – or seemingly run – the dangerous gauntlet of over-sensitivity and a form of self-absorbed state. You can see the lines of men with clubs either side of you: you think too much, you are preoccupied with yourself, you're too insular, you're too sensitive, you're over-sensitive, bash, bang wallop come the clubs reigning down on us. And because we are the way we are we really FEEL this bashing! And then we analyse the situation further and everything is exacerbated! We can't win – can we?

Why are we hard on ourselves, why do we carry the burden of being 'better'? What are we aiming for and how should we go about this?

Well of course many of us want to be better human beings but being bent over by these ideals cripples us rather than lengthens our stride. As with the MACRO it's all about what you can and can't do for yourself. What is within reach and what – we must concede – just IS. And further to this to have a sense of how we go about improving ourselves and what effect that has upon others. Maybe we'll become boring prigs. Maybe we WILL become self-obsessed and so sensitive we burn when touched.

We perceive the world inside. All our senses are perceived inside. Our brain perceives our touch, our sight, our hearing, our smell. Our reality dwells within – as does the reality of all others.

None of us here (those who are reading and myself included) want to be insensitive brutes, psychopaths, lacking in empathy and sympathy. So, we take into our reality the perceptions and realities of others. Those who touch us within. We burden ourselves with ourselves. We take on and in all the expectations of others. And in one sense this is no bad thing. We have an idea of how we SHOULD be. There is a template that runs through our lives – a mirror – of what and who we should be. And, almost inevitably, we reflect the mores and attitudes of our times. We want to be good people. We want to love and be loved. But what is the authentic us?

So many of us are struck down by mental (mind) disorder. We must 'fit in' to this society. Fit in to the expectations of others. Fit in to the – in fact – craziness of the world. We imbibe cognitive dissonance and make it our own. Inside where we dwell we carry the weight of expectation. Be young, be beautiful, be rich, be intelligent, be successful, be what I (they) want you to be. Be the ideal of family and society. Yes, and even be what you aren't! With all this pressure piling in on us is it any wonder we can't at times carry the weight. We buckle – like a horse pulling a wagon that is overloaded. No amount of whipping can ease the situation. No amount of self-flagellation can ease OUR situation.

What's to be done? The first and ancient rule is to 'know thyself'. Know who you are and what you are capable of. I recall hearing once someone saying that if there is a judgement day we will only be judged on US. It won't be a competition and comparison – but only on US. I am not saying don't try and become better or struggle for goals, but rather to understand why you are doing these things and not to carry the weight of expectation of others. Or to have unreasonable expectations of oneself. More than this to become so pressured by expectations that the weight changes you or breaks you down. We have breakdowns. We stop. We run out of petrol, the engine breaks. Beating the car (an image of Basil Fawlty forms in my mind) will do absolutely nothing. REFRAIN.

STOP – stop what you are doing and/or thinking that causes this kind of pain if nothing is achieved through it.

THINK – take time out. Find a refuge, seek asylum with a friend or family member or by oneself. Don't over-think – think plainly and honestly and simply. Or don't think at all if you're not ready.

ANALYSE – when you know what's wrong in your life or in your perceptions and attitudes – eliminate them. Or breathe into them so that they inflate for all to see and drift up and away and out of sight. Beating yourself up is a blood sport.

Be kind to yourself. Be kind to yourself even as you walk barefoot on the thorny path of perfection.

These lyrics talk about pain. Some people say, 'without pain there is no gain', but maybe pain is the wrong word. Pain makes us feel alive but in a very brutal way. When the pain is GONE – well then, we feel truly alive. Melancholia and nostalgia – they can bring a kind of sweet sorrow to life – but pain, is always painful. Maybe we need to go through pain to achieve what we want. A wise human sacrifices the present for the future. In which case choose the pain or manage the pain and don't let pain lead to annihilation. Pain is the way our body (and mind) tells us to stop what we are doing.

In the final analysis it really is about being fair with and to yourself. You are not a benign dictator of the world or a God of the world and therefore even with its best interests at heart you can only do what you can do. YOU can only DO what YOU can DO. By taking on the weight of the world (as others do) you will only let that world squash you, resulting in one (or a thousand thousand) less good people to be in the world. Be good to yourself, be good to others, do what you can. Let your energy dissipate and make the world a fraction (yes, a minute fraction) better. That is what we can do. And every time one of us does this the weight of the world really DOES get lighter! And it gets lighter for everyone.

Chapter 4

"There's still time to change the road you're on."

- 'Stairway to Heaven' – Page/Plant

Artist: Led Zeppelin. Album: Untitled but known as *Led Zeppelin IV*. Year: 1971

And indeed, there is!

Eventually our time will run out – but there is always time to change our mind and attitudes even if not the road we travel.

So, for most of us our life's road isn't that easy. There are times when we may feel like we're speeding along quite happily but before long you'll know there'll be a dense traffic jam or a must-take diversion. There are constantly traffic lights telling us when to go, stop, or wait (for what seems an eternity). There are the traffic islands (roundabouts) that see us whizzing about in no direction at all, sometimes there are peaceful country lanes (but even the peace of these can be challenged by a driver coming the other way or by a herd of cows blocking the road. Or a tractor taking its whole width).

Potholes, roadworks, angry drivers, laybys, alternate routes and service stations – don't all these seem like metaphors for life? We have maps and now sat-navs to get from A-Z and we have cars with lots of mod-cons and often quite luxurious interiors. Some of us have old cars, some motorbikes, some bicycles, some 'Shanks's pony'. We all travel along at our own pace – sometimes hurried by life – sometimes seemingly left in an eddy of backwater.

We're all on our unique journey through this life. Some feel surer about their destination than others and really seem to have their life mapped out. Maybe they allow others to dictate their route. The RAC and the AA become Christianity or Islam, say. Some even - through whichever circumstances - have others be their drivers; for instance, those who have locked-in syndrome or who are imprisoned.

We all know we're headed for the great car-park in the sky. We're all going to get there whether we drive Rolls Royces or Reliant Robins (I have owned and driven the latter!). Whether we travel a short distance or a long, whether we speed or drive slowly, whether we stop many times or take a direct route – we will get there. Thus- maybe what is important is our element of control. We have a steering wheel. An accelerator, a brake. We can indicate our intentions. We can look at the road ahead and glance in our rear-view mirror. We can engage the clutch and disengage the engine. Or we can walk steadily along as others shoot past us.

What IS the road that you are on? Have you chosen your road? Are you there by default or by bad signposting? Were you diverted some way back? Do you feel this is the right road for you – or should you be on another type of surface travelling through other landscapes or cityscapes?

We must know HOW we are travelling (which mode of transport) and why we are on the road we are on. And we need to have some idea of why we are on the route we appear to be on. You see we could have hopped on a coach or train, and just sat back and watched the fields, towns, clouds roll by.

Life's road can seem so hard at times. A steep never-ending hill. Hitch-hikers begging for us to pick them up. Luggage weighing down on the car's roof. Potholes shaking the suspension. And though we try to suspend disbelief at our metaphorical journey we are jolted into the realisation that fuel is running out. It constantly runs out. Can we make it to the next petrol station? Can we make it home?

However we propel ourselves, there is some energy that is needed. There are other travellers even on the loneliest of roads. There are always accidents waiting to happen. But there is also the beauty of the open-road, of the sunken lane, of the wild mountain track, of the straight highway where we can speed for a while, of the breath-taking open-roofed sportster or the low-slung motorbike so sensitive to the turn of our wrist. There is the euphoria of free-wheeling down a hill on a bicycle. The freedom of being on foot. The care-free ride of a planned journey on a train. And we can – ALWAYS – turn off the road we're on or get off the train or bus or out of the taxi we have paid for.

Let's look how we might change the road we're on and what we'll need to do this. I mean it's simple to change direction isn't it? Well, yes and no. But we always CAN! Often, we say we are 'stuck in a rut', I had that exact experience when I was driving one of my Reliant Robins. These are curious three-wheeled cars with fibre-glass bodies. It had snowed heavily one winter where I used to live and as ever cars had left many channels in the snow, other cars following these 'ruts'. But my car was different it had the single front wheel, if I followed a channel I was completely caught in it and my rear wheels were free but struggling. The single wheel could not turn out of the rut and forge new ones like the other cars. I was trapped in the direction of others. I was driving along the route of another car without the possibility of getting out! How often do we feel like that?! Our way has been made by those who came before us or who are stronger than us.

Changing road, changing direction can be risky – like overtaking! But you can do it. You might feel that the life mapped out before you doesn't suit you, doesn't really reflect who you are. Turning onto another road could mean:

- Changing career
- Changing location
- Changing partner
- Changing religion
- Changing politics
- Changing how we lead/view life
- Changing something in ourselves
- Changing the nature of the way we lead our life
- Changing our morals/attitudes
- Changing our body
- Changing how we perceive our life
- Changing how we relate to others

No doubt there are many other changes. It's one thing to say yes you can change road (which you can) and making that turn. But look at that list. All those changes can be made. The consequences of the new road you take and what its surface is like will depend on many things. What is fundamental is the DECISION to change. Honestly, you could crash as you take that turning too fast or at the last minute, so again, it's the decision – how and when and why you take it – that truly counts.

Don't be diverted by picking up that mobile and using it while you drive. You know you shouldn't. And it's distracting you from the road. Keep communications focussed. Keep in mind where YOU are going. Okay you can pick up a hitch-hiker – give someone a helping hand, if they're on the same journey.

Music helps you along too, or an audio book. Music and writing can help you on your journey, can even BE the journey. But keep focussed.

As with everything in this life first comes the internal decision to wish to change, and then the decision TO change. You must make that first. Pick up the map, re-set the sat-nav, DREAM. Once you have made the decision then plot your course. To get from A-Z on another road you're going to have to have the right vehicle and to know the terrain, know where the stops are. But the first thing is simply to make the turning.

I believe once we decide the Universe becomes subtly aware of this and helps direct us, it may not smooth out the way – but it acknowledges our determination and drive to our new destination.

Whichever turning you take, be kind. If you must drop folk off or wave them goodbye – be kind. We have this one life and we MUST direct ourselves and be comfortable with what we drive (or how we walk/cycle) and understand the way we set off and move. Everything we do is an expression of us. Leaving behind those who take different routes might be necessary. We can keep waving as they disappear. We can also encourage others either to understand the route we need to take or to help them encourage us. We can't dictate the way of others. Even if we share the same bus or train this is all voluntary, and if we feel we ARE being driven against our will then we need to do all we can to STOP-GET OFF and find our own way.

Yes, it's easier said than done. The road might seem long and twisting into the darkness ahead. The road might peter out into a rough-track, or drop down into dense woodland, or skirt the side of a mountain, or tunnel darkly into a rock face. It takes nerve to drive ourselves at times.

Driving is a skill. It requires independence and to be independent when necessary. Keep fixed on your destination, they say it's the travelling that counts, and so it may well be. But it's good to keep that light shining over the destination line. We might not get there but WE have taken the decision to change, to turn, to be at one with our inner transport.

Turning is:
- The writing of a letter to a new company, a place of education – for a new career. Or handing in your notice. One car comes to a screeching halt, but we just KNOW another has to (and will) come along.
- Putting the beloved house up for sale, with all its memories. But we don't necessarily want or need to stay in the same place.
- Tenderly parting company from someone with whom, deep-down, it isn't working. We would be fooling ourselves and perhaps more importantly – them – for carrying on.
- Changing our faith, we may have grown up in a religion but what is right for us might lie somewhere else within a different spirituality.

Being able to step out from the crowd and say: I support this person or this party. Maybe facing hostility and ridicule.

Becoming closer to the person we view ourselves as, thus surrounding ourselves with other like-minded folk, going to different places. Even being alone – if this is what we choose.

Maybe stopping a habit. A way of being. We are often perceived by what we do AND what we have done. We are not anyone's hostage. Especially not hostage to our past. We can be - and do that which is - truer to ourselves.

We could take up a long-cherished hobby that puts us on a different road peopled by very different fellow travellers/passengers.

We could BE someone different to the expectations of both others and ourselves. A desire to change the world begins with the need to change ourselves.
We could change our outward appearance (but accept that this might not be a root cause of our unhappiness or desire for change).

We could decide to re-evaluate who we are and our self-concept. Just the way we view who WE are and our relationship with others could bring about huge change. We live 'within' though often confuse the 'outside' with reality. By changing our perception, we can certainly change our reality. Or begin that change!

We can learn to communicate with others differently. Change our mind-set, our set mind. Books, music, travelling can all broaden the mind. The same neurons that we use to experience a sunset are the ones we use to hear a bird call. We are the providers of our life and its reality. Our neurons are where all reality exists. BUT – we must use those very neurons to take the turning. We – this consciousness – has that ability. Turn and watch the road and all about it change.

Remember when you first learnt to drive (if indeed you did) – how it all seemed so complicated, with limbs used for this and that, how could we do it? And then to control this huge hunk of metal and its powerful engine. But we did. Or do. Or might. With POWER we also have BRAKES, with SPEED we also have a STEERING wheel, we can change GEAR. We are in control, but we must learn HOW. Eventually it all becomes smooth and natural. And when the sun shines on the road ahead and we feel awake and in control then it is sublime to let our sub-conscious drive as we take in the world's surrounding, natural beauty.

If the road ahead meets obstacles. Then we shall drive round them, even if it means turning back for a while. Even if holding a map in our hand and DREAMING of where we will travel is the most we can do, then at least we CAN dream. All of us can dream. We need to dream. Dreams refresh the mind.

If you need to, if you know so, make the decision to change roads. You still have time to change. And you always will.

Chapter 5

"All the money you made/Will never buy back your soul."

- 'Masters of War' - Bob Dylan

Artist: Bob Dylan. Album: *The Freewheelin' Bob Dylan*. Year: 1963

When Bob sings this he is assuming – that you have lost your soul. And further he explicitly suggests that it has been through the acquisition of money. In making all that money you lost your soul in the process. Money became your God; your spiritual path; your primary desire. Of course, I'm second-guessing. I'm looking at this lyric and taking it as it is – standing alone. Let us look at the truths and implications.

We all need money to survive, (I talk generally, and it seems to apply throughout most cultures/nations in the world). Bob isn't talking about this aspect. Exchanging money (effectively promissory notes) for deeds done or goods sold is the way of the world. For most of us we receive just about enough money with which to survive, there is a balance between what we earn (or get) and what we spend, most of us probably over-spend somewhat – it's hard not to. We are held in the grip of loans and mortgages. Mortgage comes from the amalgamation of the French words meaning dead and guarantee (or wager).

So, Bob talking generally, maybe about those he knows very well, maybe about himself – is talking about a different relationship with money. Filthy lucre. He's talking about selling our integrity, our spirit, our heart, our essence for that which brings only material gain. (I have the impression he's not talking about great philanthropic folk here as their very philanthropy would maintain their spirit.) Bob has been immersed in the music BUSINESS for a very long time. And he has had ample chance to see up close what the pursuit of money can do to people. I say he might be talking about himself too (or all of us) in the sense that this is also a specific warning. It's an indictment for sure but I think it acts as a stark warning (and especially in his circles where there still IS money to be made).

I don't think you can separate the acquisition of money from power either. The two come hand in hand. What else is excess money for? How many cars, boats, planes do you need to buy?

There's something else in this lyric too. The explicit statement of what money CANNOT buy. It can't buy BACK your soul. That indicates that there is no redemption. If you've lost your soul to greed, then that's it. Well – in fact – more specifically it means THE MONEY can't buy back your soul! But those who have worshipped the 'green back' still can be redeemed. As can we all.

Let's wind this down to our ordinary level, we might have money, we might be in a considerable amount of debt. What's important to us (and especially to our soul) is our relationship with money. How we relate to those paper notes and what we expect of them. We need money. We need food and shelter, we need to pay bills – it's the way of the world. Money can't buy you love (as a famous group once sang!), it can buy you attention and sex of course – but not love. It can't buy someone's SOUL!

Money lies at the root of our perceptions of our place in this world. If you work for free you aren't seemingly valued in the same way as doing the same job for money! It's almost as if the more you charge the more you are valued. Perhaps even the more you value yourself! People's perceptions of you and what you produce are altered by an impression of value.

People generally strive for wealth, often understandably because money and savings bring comfort and security. Poverty isn't pleasurable. There is the adage that when poverty knocks at the door love leaves by the window. Poverty is a destroyer – of everything. Many of us dread slipping into this state. This is reasonable and understandable. Not all seem to be at risk of course.

Some of us accrue wealth for the status it brings. We are not concerned with our spiritual development, maybe not even our cultural enrichment, this is conspicuous consumption. Look at me! Look at how well I'm doing. I'm doing so much better than you! The UK has a comedian, Harry Enfield, who had a character

Loadsamoney who flaunted his wealth, and another character whose catch phrase was: 'Because I'm considerably richer than you!' This was the pleasure they took. Being richer than other folk. They derived much enjoyment and pleasure from this. And we all know people who really like to flaunt their wealth.

But when it comes time to die, to move on from this life, what will their money and actions resulting from excess wealth bring them then? They may well say – well, this is the only life there is, we will perish at death, our personality will be annihilated. So, who cares? We had fun, We did what we wanted, money bought us everything we wanted. They could be right. And they could of course, be very wrong.

If there is no life beyond this then THIS life is certainly the most important expression of our conscious being. Evidently. We find ourselves born and raised in the world of our time. Then we have decisions to be made throughout our experience on Planet Earth. You, me, they – all have decisions, sometimes choices. How we decide and choose defines us as the people we are.

People go to extremes to gain money, and money for the sake of money. I know this from observations in real life. They will do anything (and I mean ANYTHING) for more green-backs. What has happened to them? What has so distorted their life view.

We need to balance our life and balance our attitude towards money. A friend of mine joined the Hare Krishna movement and became something of a 'big wig' – and good luck to him. I was dropped as a friend because I didn't follow the same path. That was a pity. But I recall him saying to me that there was nothing wrong with material possession (and by default the money that acquired it) but rather what was important was how it was used. The purpose to which it was put. And he was right.

Money must not become our Godhead, for in that we would truly lose our soul. We come into this world with nothing and so shall we leave. And we need to keep recalling this – and in a genuinely celebratory way. But we also need to be kind to ourselves. Be kind to others. If we have money – spend it wisely, joyfully, give it away. Help others. Remember too the 'widow's mite' where she gave so little, but this was – in effect – so much.

Do you remember the marvellous story by Charles Dickens: *'A Christmas Carol'*? What a wonderful story of redemption and a life turned around from the worship of money to the joyous worship of love of his fellows. 'Scrooge' is not an insult – it is to be named after a man who through repentance and a change of heart became a glorious giving human being. Before this change money had indeed poisoned and lost him his soul. But through giving money away and sharing with others the same money (previously jealously hoarded) became a great force for good. It is what you DO with it that counts. It's how and why you obtain it that counts.

Bob Dylan admonishes those he believes have lost their soul to the acquisition of money. And he taunts with his warning, this money will not buy back your soul. For the soul of us is not to be bought or sold. WE are not to be bought or sold. No amount of money can buy back a soul that has been driven out by greed. We must change for our soul to inhabit us once again, should we fall servant to the Money God.

How much money do we need? What is the balance between the spiritual nature to our lives and our needs as organic beings? What is sufficient? Having money gives us the power to spend, to redirect, to aid. It gives us the power over others at times. We can buy and sell lives. Most of us simply get by. It is perhaps a curse to have so much money. To walk down a street and see a beggar and to KNOW that you could change his life. Or it's a blessing to know that you have more money than needed and can give to others and change their lives beyond belief.

On a smaller scale, giving a little to those who really need it is such a beautiful gift. A friend of mine recently gave me a small amount of money (but an amount that helped me and made me feel so blessed) as he knew that I was somewhat in need (though of course there are those in MORE need). He recalled that I had helped him out some years previously, I had forgotten this. I just helped him out because I could and these years later he helped me out – because he could. Nothing grand, and yet, perfect. And now we are bonded by our mutual giving.

There is a saying: 'Neither a lender nor a borrower be'. There's empirical wisdom in that, an adage handed down through the ages. It is better to give unconditionally. Not to expect a return and yet a return may come (and it may not). This is not about anyone else but YOU. Having money in excess is - as said – to have a continual opportunity, an opportunity to buy, to give, to hoard, to share. An opportunity and a burden.

For all those with wealth and success – what does it buy them in the end? Have they allowed the power of money to pervert their soul? Do you have to be a beggar to have pure spirituality? Do you need to give until it hurts? We aren't saints, we struggle along in this world, we try to do our best. We must maintain ourselves and our families, we can't give to the poorest and watch our own suffer. All we can do is spend our money wisely. And pay attention to our soul.

What is our soul? This word/idea 'soul' is of course the absolute crux of Dylan's lyric. Our essence? Our integrity? The mystical part of us that we can only glance at from the corner of an eye? Revelation made manifest within? An idea of godhead that keeps surfacing in our consciousness? The feeling we have when walking in nature? An inkling that we are more than just body? Uncanny experiences? Belief in the supernatural within us? Goodness within? Energy passed between bodies?

Can soul be linked to the mundane? To materialism? To MONEY? *'For what shall it profit a man, if he shall gain the whole world, and lose his own soul?'*

I am lucky to have the passion of music within me, if I make money I spend anything left-over on better equipment so that I can produce better music. And, I hope, touch people's soul. A constant ebbing and flowing of money. Many of us direct our money towards our children. This is natural. Again, the money flows. Direct money through necessity and love – you can't go far wrong!

A friend of mine said: Happiness and contentment are found in small things – not money!

That's perhaps the final paradox – those that have an excess of money cease to find happiness through it. Hence, they come to a point of 'lacking' (it is their soul that lacks). And at this point they spend more – like a gambler who keeps gambling to get his money back, and like the gambler, they just lose more.

Your money is your own, and if produced through honest toil and hard work it is for you to decide what you do with it. All that is required is that money does not become your master. That is all that is required. Do not worship money or the power and material possessions it brings you. Enjoy your money in an easy, honest and sharing way. If you have little money, persevere, don't sell your soul or even your dignity to get it. If it is money to survive and/or help dependents, then ask out loud that it might come to you – not for your selfish needs. And wait. Keep trusting. Do what you must do for your sake and others.

For those of you who have much money, please consider its effect upon you and others. Be aware of any manipulation, any loss of soul (feeling, integrity, love). In the end WHO you are is so much more important than WHAT you own.

You can have money and be a good, honest person. It really isn't about money itself – that is but wads of paper. It is about YOU!

Chapter 6

"In the burning heart
Just about to burst
There's a quest for answers
An unquenchable thirst."

- 'Burning Heart' - Jim Peterik / Frank Sullivan

Artist: Survivor (Used on the *Rocky IV Soundtrack*).
Year: 1985

The burning heart, the heart of something, your heart. Pressure built to bursting, raging fire. Heart, passion, intensity. Beating, expanding – ready to explode! Pain, discomfort, emotional excess.

What is the heart? The opening line: *What do you think of in the burning heart?* - suggests what are your thoughts as calamity (or an absolute INTENSITY) strikes. The heart may well feel it's getting hotter and hotter, burning inside you – your skin dehydrating. Your heart palpitating. What do you think of then? It taunts. It feels accusatory in the sense that – this is the moment of truth! The end of something that has been heated with the friction of a thousand drum beats, NOW what will you think about. It's as if you are the cause of this. Examine yourself! Your heart pounds with such intensity you are forced to face yourself. Face whatever it is that burns inside.

But the whole thing gets turned with the lyrics: *There's a quest for answers* [noble or futile in pursuit] *an unquenchable thirst*. The heart is near exploding but even at one's most passionate or violent or amid passion and violence – answers are still required! Thus, when something has been detonated, quickened and heat radiated, and all feels like it is about to burst and explode – even then – there is the age-old quest for answers!

Is this an admonishment to control one's thoughts? Or to refine one's thoughts? Or to be mindful? Maybe it's your mind that's about to burst. With the striking of a thousand thoughts! The pressure is on, the pressure that will blow, you are under pressure, feeling the strain, feeling the intensity, what are your thoughts at this time? Questions? Are you seeking answers even as all seems likely to spontaneously combust? Is that the human condition? Did the human condition bring about this calamity? Do we need this kind of intensity?

Let us consider the point, the centre of the calamity – the moment before bursting. The heart of darkness, the final coming together to blast everything apart. At this moment how must you think. Must you think?

Do we tend to lose our heads when disaster strikes? Do we over-analyse? Even at bursting point we are unquenchable in our desire for answers. O how human is this. In the heart of this calamity our own heart pulses, quickens, pumps blood through our body. We are flooded with adrenaline, fight or flight? Our brain is white-hot with thought. Action. We must know everything, we must have answers, the flames are rising, eating at the soles of our feet, sweat pours off us and our palms are wet. And we want answers. Noble or futile?

At a point where everything has speeded up (with our pulse) we seek answers. The heart of everything is burning. And we rail against fate! What are we supposed to do? We are human. Humans seek answers in adversity. We must know what is happening to us, surely?

We walk in the searing heat of the desert, we are lost. We are in the burning heart of the land of dunes and grit. Our heart is trying to keep us alive, to regulate our temperature, to create equilibrium. The sun pulses above us leeching out all moisture. We are becoming as dry rags fluttering in a flaming breeze. What do we think? What is important to us?

These are not the thoughts of the old who sleep before an open-fire. This is raging intensity, we feel our gums melting, we are close to bursting from within. What do we think?

Our heart is burning, and we are unquenchable in our thirst for answers, or we are in the heart of something close to bursting and we quest answers. The human spirit and its quest for knowledge is unquenchable. When we are close to bursting or all around us burns we still seek out answers. Maybe at these times of calamity or an overload of events (passion maybe) that

IS the time to seek answers. What brought us into or to this state? Can we tame the burning – or do we even wish to?

Fire begins with a flash, a struck match, a lightning bolt, a friction, the flames leap and are newly born into the rich air that feeds them. If left untended the flames will roll out like a tidal wave – burning all before, a scorching bush fire, raging, out-of-control, intense and moving, laying waste to all that fuels it - leaving desolation, (and yet clears out the old and prepares for the new). It has no reason but to eat all before it. And then the fire becomes embers. In the embers we find contemplation and imagination, a play of pulsating colour, the flames are died down, there is an intensity, but it is warming and reassuring.

Each of these stages is like our thoughts over time. The energetic strike of sulphur as a match is scraped into life. A small explosion of light and heat. Potential. The essence of genius, or creativity, we must tend this little flame and feed it, without material to burn and the air to combust with, the little flame will quickly die, and with it all possibility. We have an idea for a story, a piece of music, a hobby, a business, a thought to share, an insight, feed it or 'puff' - it is gone.

If we allow our thoughts to run free we can be overwhelmed as a forest fire burns across the neurons of our brain. Too many thoughts, confusing, so much information to fan the flames, so hot and fast we cannot control these thoughts, they burn us, destroy us, we are fed into a maelstrom of ideas and information and there is so much fire and heat that we are often left in the desolation of its passing. What happened? Where does that leave us? Or like a situation that got out of hand – we become a burnt survivor.

When our passions are cooled slightly we can investigate the embers for wisdom. There we can reflect upon the life of a fire that links us all and takes us back to those first humans that controlled the flame. Those first humans that gained power over all else but also those first humans that reflected in the darkness sitting round their camp's fire, or in a cave with the last flames and shadows flickering on the stone walls. The beginnings of conversation and ideas shared. Where philosophy was born.

You have an unquenchable quest for answers. It is understandable and natural. But don't let these thoughts consume you. Control the flames that rage inside, wait for them to smoulder and spit and glow and illuminate deeply. Don't let your heart burst seeking answers.

Your heart is the passionate, caring, feeling side, and sometimes it burns with pain and anger and frustration. And LOVE & DESIRE!

Can we think straight when our heart is fit to burst? As our pulse quickens we perceive time differently, time slows - we speed. And in this moment a vast army of thoughts can troop down into our mind. We are tuned into a higher state maybe. At this point we need to marshal ideas and keep as calm and as balanced as we possibly can.

Some would say that our search for questions at times of stress or calamity is a foolish Human thing to do. Maybe they are right, but it IS very human. We are natural explorers of the land and MIND! And maybe these moments of stress bring insight. And aren't we natural survivors?

Whatever befalls you know that it is natural to seek answers. Sometimes no answers will come – no matter how our heart burns. If you can find inner stillness and peace you are truly blessed. There are ways to achieve equilibrium through meditation and yoga. If this doesn't suit you then you can find time stilling when you paint or make music or write words on a page.

Take a piece of paper and write down everything that enters your head. These words are YOUR words. Let them go. Leave them. Come back to them. Read from yourself to yourself. The simple act of filling the blank page with your words is therapeutic – that I can guarantee.

Go to an art shop and buy a cheap canvas and some pastel crayons. Draw something. Anything. Colour the drawing as you wish. Now rub the colours in – watch them blend. Concentrate on the colours and form. As you get into this you'll find yourself liberated. Free of time and free of worry. You won't be able to help yourself. No-one needs to know about this or see what you have done. It's YOURS, it belongs to you and has come out of you at this time.

Pick up a guitar (or go out and buy a cheap one). Get it tuned – we all know someone who plays. Strike a string and listen. Chords are just several strings held down by fingertips at the same time, and strummed, plucked, stroked. The act of learning and playing and listening will liberate you from both time and worry.

All these things can be done for ten minutes or longer – it doesn't matter too much as in DOING them you will be liberated. It will ease the burning sensation for moments of time. And it will clear your mind.

If none of these appeals, then walk into the countryside, (catch a bus there/drive/cycle). Simply by walking we create a rhythm and nature adds the harmony that is absent from a city or town. Away from all stress and information you can again escape the tumbling thoughts. As you walk your mind will clear – as if by magic. Your pace will be rhythmic. You'll hear everything around and see the greenery and colours of nature. Being IN this real world but OUT of the information-load 'reality' of your existence will give perspective. Distance. Contemplation. Just a walk can make you feel so much better. And the questions you so long to ask will form and often be answered. Because your mind has time and space to answer. **Everything is found within you. YOU are the creator.**

You are the creator (or the receiver) of your thoughts. You are the mind that answers (or receives answers). Don't let your heart be consumed by painful fire. Find escape from time and from the incessant pressure of the moment. Like a play on repeat you CAN choose to leave by the wings, things still go on and the actors will be the same. But you can watch from the sides or the stalls, or the royal box! You can – in moments of timelessness – move between the actors as if they have stood still. You can also write part of all their scripts as well as your own.

If your heart bursts with pain – you will survive. Because your heart cannot be destroyed. It will serve you throughout your life.

And throughout your life you will search for answers, and that's a beautiful preoccupation. Keep asking the questions. Keep writing your script. Be creative. Step out of time. Be kind to yourself. Love your life.

YOU are the creator.

Just remember that.

Take your crayon, or keypad, or pencil, or brush, or guitar, or drum, or harmonica, or lift your legs and walk, and be timeless for a while.

Chapter 7

"What a wicked game you played to make me feel this way
What a wicked thing to do to let me dream of you
What a wicked thing to say you never felt this way
What a wicked thing to do to make me dream of you."

-'Wicked Game' - Chris Isaak

Artist: Chris Isaak. Album: *Heart Shaped World*. Year: 1989

And it is as if we are but the puppets of other people. It is what YOU did, what YOU said, how YOU made us feel and dream! But of course, it isn't is it?

In a 'one-way' relationship it seems we are the manipulated ones. Not only are we manipulated but it has been done in a thoroughly 'wicked' way. You were the sorcerer or sorceress that cast your spell. A magical cupid who we could not resist. And then once having captured our heart and soul you deny your very feelings. You MUST have these feelings for us surely?! How could you not! Then we are left to dream of you and even our dreams are orchestrated by your wickedness.

It has nothing to do with US of course. It is all YOU. YOU have all the power – it seems.

We must face reality. We can NEVER force someone to love us, to feel as we do about them. This is a difficulty that so many of us fail to understand. Isn't that how love works? We fall in love with someone so surely by osmosis they must fall in love with us? Otherwise how can we feel this love? If we love you – you must therefore love us. It's a simple equation. If our love for you is genuine then it must be reciprocated. If it is not reciprocated, then we must have been beguiled, beguiled by the other who refuses to return our feelings.

Part of growing up is to understand that what we feel may not be universal. It stems from the 'giving to receive' principle. The selfish love principle. Look at me,

I am everything you want and need therefore you cannot possibly not want me. I give - you receive - and you give back. That's how we think the world operates. But of course, it doesn't. As we mature we understand that the world does NOT revolve around us.

You cannot force someone to FEEL in the way you expect them to. These people are not projections of your own being and doing, they are complicated human beings with all the baggage that human beings often seem to carry. We expect reactions and sentiments that comply with our feelings and sentiments. It is naive and immature of us to expect so. Whether we like it or not we have to acknowledge the autonomy of other people. Yet don't we truly feel 'in love'? Doesn't it hurt so much? This is real! How can it feel real if it's not reciprocated? You can only know this when you're in deep, fully immersed in sentiment and feeling.

The first thing we need to do – is STOP our projections. Whatever we may/may not feel and however our feelings are being responded to – we MUST stop attributing ideas/thoughts/motivations to those we are 'in love' with. This the primary step. If nothing else this will be fair and just on the person we purport to feel so much for. So...unless we know otherwise, for certain, DO NOT project. We might expect them to behave in a certain manner – if they don't, then accept that as their genuine reaction. Of course, there are many GAMES played in flirtation and the opening steps of LOVE. We don't want to curtail the *pas-de-deux* of a burgeoning relationship. Courtship is a complicated and subtle dance. It has inherent dangers of loss and unrequited attention. That is what makes it so full of frisson and passion. But if someone doesn't love you that's when the game must finish. We must end the game, the pretence, the unrequited nature with dignity and integrity.

When we are, or feel we are, in love we can become quite selfish. Sting might have written: *'If you love somebody set them free'*, but there seems a tendency to capture and keep hold of our obsession. It's natural. We want what we want and many of us are used to having what we want. But thankfully in these days, owning people is unlawful! People's affections cannot be bought. The laws of attraction and repulsion apply to us and them and there's not much we can do about that. I know that some people believe money CAN buy you love, but it's not really love they're buying. It seems for some that wealth and good looks help facilitate the 'falling in love business', but isn't that just a tiny bit wicked?

We want genuine affection, genuine feelings, genuine reciprocation of our feelings. And the only way we can have that is to be ourselves. To be true. To be authentic. To be genuine. To know what the true nature of love is. To know ourselves. And we can NEVER know YOU in the way we know US!

There's rarely any wickedness in others not wishing to love us, and if there was we'd be better off without them. We reflect our emotions upon those we hold up before us to be adored. We put them on the age-old pedestal. We furnish them with attributes as a playwright embellishes a sketched-out character. Let's concentrate on us first. Let us get ourselves and our relationship with ourselves right to begin with. If we are happy with how we are and understand where we relate to our emotions, then not only will we interact with others more effectively, but we will begin to understand the nature of GENUINE relationships. **We need to know who we are to understand who others are,**

we need to be sure of the truth of our own feelings before we can attract that truth in others.

So many people chase love, so many people blame those they love for failing them in some way. They even blame those they purport to love for not loving back. How cruel is that? That can't be love. Yes, it's cruel that seemingly genuine feelings aren't mirrored. But that's life. What is needed is clear sight and understanding. And selflessness. There IS also the need to keep the magical and mystical element of falling in love too. It isn't a mathematical equation. If he has this or she has that then all will be well, love isn't a mathematical equation, a set of values, a tick-box list. There must be an element that transcends the ordinary. We can date on-line, we can go on blind-dates, no problem. But falling in love is something unforeseeable. There are those who believe that love can grow too. That might be the case, but if it IS the case then BOTH people will allow that love to grow between them. No-one can ever be forced into love. It will not and cannot work. And sometimes people seem to 'fall out' of love too. There is nothing that can be done about that either but be who we are and maintain ourselves and our dignity and integrity.

Maybe it's a kind of paranoia that descends upon us when we fall for someone. We do seem to get blinded to reality. The person of our affections can become god-like in their relevance to us and our life. So, take a step back. Please understand that the most important thing is to be you and only you. No-one or nothing else. Be you. Wearing masks might seem efficient at the time – but one day your true face WILL be revealed.

Being yourself is a gift to yourself. If love is to blossom, then you need to be authentic and trust that the person you love has learnt to be authentic too. But their authenticity is beyond your control. Knowing and understanding yourself will help you to know and understand the person you love. Perhaps the most difficult thing is to step back from this opening relationship whilst still feeling all the wonderful feelings you would expect from someone (such as yourself) who is in love. The stepping back though is only to be true to your self - and expecting nothing from the person of your desires and affections. That is all you need to do. Be true to yourself and expect nothing from the other.

Courtship is a kind of game, it is necessary in a civilised society. The rules are subtle, but the courtship dance is to be enjoyed. This dance can be rushed or by-passed, but it is essential to be taken authentically. The dance allows the other to express themselves in their own time, if it is you who is leading. If it is the other who takes the lead it allows you to respond and mirror in your own good time. There is no wickedness in this dance only the frisson of expectation as each move is revealed. How many people have cast aside this subtle dance for the immediacy of lust? And in so doing, of course, they have revealed the lack of authentic love.

We may ask what love is and what guides our feelings. And we may never reach a reasoned comprehensive argument. But what we can know is how WE feel. What this means to US. Even if we descend into paranoia or the heady feelings of unrequited love (and its sweet pain) then as long as we know our feelings and do not punish those who have rejected our feelings then all will pass. They say that all is fair in love and war. It is both fair and unfair of course. It is fair when we ask nothing of the other. And when they ask nothing of us.

Shakespeare wrote in his 'Sonnet 116'

Love is not love
Which alters when it alteration finds,
Or bends with the remover to remove.
O no! it is an ever-fixed mark

We must think of love as a mystical force that binds us. A force that seeks out two people when those two people are both ready and accepting of its binding power.

Don't let yourself be so in love that you drown within its waters. Or be so vulnerable that your openness is mocked or taken advantage of. Again – be clear, be true and be yourself. Enjoy your feelings but acknowledge the authenticity of others. If they treat you cruelly that is NOT an expression of love. If they take advantage of you – that is NOT an expression of love. We are all complicated beings, and nothing runs smoothly, so accept imperfections (of course). Do not assume the thoughts or motivations of others. If love is there to blossom it will do so. LET love flourish and blossom, NEVER force yourself or the other into love. Again – step back. Enjoy the feelings. Ask yourself: Am

I being me? Am I being authentic? Am I allowing the other to be themselves with no imposed expectations?

Love isn't – or certainly shouldn't be – complicated, although we as humans are complicated. All around us people are searching for love, and others are falling out of love. Some find love, and some seem to look so hard they never do. Like a flower we can but open ourselves to the bee that seeks us out. Or be the bee that finds the flower that has opened itself. When you stop looking – then you find!

It is YOU who feels the way you do.
It is YOU who dreams of your loved one.
It is YOUR feelings that are authentic, and you cannot force the other to be anything other than what they are. If they have lied to you – that is their inauthentic behaviour. In revealing this, they have allowed you freedom.

Enjoy your dreams. Enjoy the way you feel. Go in with an open heart. Be yourself. If love is there it will flow. Allow the other to reveal themselves and their true nature. Enjoy the dance.

- Thank the one you love for the way they have made you feel and the dreams they have inspired! And enjoy your dreams. Be authentic!

Chapter 8

"Don't it always seem to go/That you don't know what you've got till it's gone."

- 'Big Yellow Taxi' – Joni Mitchell

Artist: Joni Mitchell. Album: *Ladies of the Canyon* Year:1970

Decisions, decisions, decisions.

I seem to recall reading the idea that at every moment in life there is the potential for unlimited possibilities, as if the universe is born anew to us at that very moment. In fact, that latter idea sprang into my mind as I typed. The fraction of a moment before I typed – was that the universe presenting itself with limitless possibilities? Is that where creative acts come from? Further – is there such a thing as a conscious present?!

Let us assume there is a 'present' wherein we can make decisions relating to our lives. And thus, as the present unfolds we continue to make – if you like – micro, or mundane decisions. Have a cup of tea. Open the window. Draw the face of a cat. Clean the car. Many of the things we do we aren't conscious of, this operating at the bodily level: breathing/heart-beating/maintaining bodily temperature/scratching a leg. When we drive a car – for the most part we aren't conscious of what we're doing. We can BECOME conscious, depending on circumstances – but often we are driving without thinking, have you ever begun driving to X only to find you're on your way to work, the same journey that you make every day? Something snaps you out of your sub-conscious state and then you consciously drive the car in the right direction. As a musician I play my best music when I don't let thinking get in my way.

Here I am floating the idea that there are conscious and sub-conscious decisions made. Constantly being made. Most of these decisions are automatic (BREATHE!) and/or at a very micro level. Some decisions are well thought out and HIGHLY conscious and affect our lives in a very MACRO way. The BIG decisions in life - life-changing decisions. Life constantly changing as we move through our perception of 'time'. We look in the mirror and see change.

We make decisions that affect our life and others make decisions that affect our life. The world continues its path and we are affected at various levels. Throughout all of this we maintain the sensation – for the most part – that we are autonomous and un-changing. Because the big decisions are few and far between (for most of us) and the smaller, micro decisions take care of themselves, we are lulled into a sense of false security. Everything seems to be going along just fine. Or, everything seems to be tolerable. And then – BANG! Something has changed. Something has such an impact on our life that it changes our conscious perception of life itself and our perception of our selves.

This is felt most keenly when someone close to us ceases to be part of our life. Someone walks out on a relationship with us. A family member dies. A friend moves abroad. A club we belong to dissolves. Okay there are grades of impact here. So, let me first describe the action and its effect and then take some examples. We are severed from some valued or loving relationship. We feel this keenly and are deeply affected. We feel abandoned. And one of the reactions is then to UNDERSTAND what this relationship meant to us. We truly did NOT know what we had – until we lost it.

Let's take a close friend who moves away – a long way away. We have grown up with this friend and they have become 'part of our life'. Naturally, and easily, a part of our life. We can count on them. A relaxed relationship – a relationship that just IS. It's almost as if they have been with us all throughout our lives. It's a given. It's normal for us. Why would anything change? But a change has come. Our friend, taking a decision for themselves – a BIG decision - is moving abroad and starting a new life. This comes as a shock. There's a kind of denial. Everything remains the same until the very moment they have gone. Goodbyes are said – it's almost surreal. The last time you see them, yet it's almost like it's any other time, any other moment of saying 'goodbye'. And then they're gone.

When someone has gone far away it's almost as if they have died, yes you can call them on the phone, Skype, communicate through social media, but you suddenly realise how much you needed them close, and conveniently, by. How much you miss them. At this level of understanding you can appreciate just how much you relied upon them - how much you took them for granted. How much you needed their company and how much you cared for them. Only when they were no longer there did you learn to value them fully.

When someone you love has died and there's no real hope of communication (though, as stated previously, I do not rule out some form of possible post-death communication) then you really are left to comprehend and come to terms with this gaping hole in your life. If you CAN comprehend. If you can come to terms. How is it that when someone close has died you are not only filled with grief but there comes a feeling of guilt too. You didn't know what you truly had until that person, that relationship, was severed completely. All that love was taken for granted. Taken for granted because it was easily and naturally given.

Implicit in these lyrics is both the sense of loss and the understanding and awareness that comes after the loss. And, that you didn't fully comprehend what you had. With the loss comes a 'coming to one's senses'. Now we must ask and reflect upon the nature of the relationship that is lost. A bereavement is the most extreme form of course. How can we redeem ourselves from our past actions when no future actions are possible? Well, what we can do is use 'loss' to change us for the good.

If we have behaved badly or selfishly with someone no longer with us – then the loss of them and our understanding of that loss and how much we TRULY valued them must change us at a deep, fundamental level. Recall that we are constantly making decisions – micro and macro, the important decisions are the ones we need to change. From this point on you can alter ANY relationship you have with ANYBODY. It may be a cliché but it's okay to tell someone how much you value them. How can, say, telling someone you love them be embarrassing for them (and if you think it might, then find another way of expressing your love)? You might feel embarrassment at the time but that will be nothing compared with the comprehension of how much they meant to you when they have gone and that you didn't say what was necessary while they still lived.

It's also about being AWARE. Being aware of yourself and your relations with others. If you DO know what you've got, then there will be no shocking surprise when the person you love leaves your side. Being aware means, you are always in a mindful relationship. You don't need to go overboard about this. You don't need to shower your girl (or boy) friend with flowers and chocolates every day. As a man I'm not sure what I would, or have, expected from girlfriends in the past. I think I was embarrassed receiving flowers once. (Well I like flowers wild in meadows and heathland and in rocky outcrops and on hill or mountainsides.) But you get the point. It's a question of valuing those in your life and making the most of your relationship with them. What more can we do? To be at ease with someone is truly liberating.

You don't know what you've got till it's gone? Well now we must try to really know. Also, we need to be aware that nothing and no-one is 'forever'.

These lyrics also speak to me of being aware of the beauty that surrounds us, isn't it easy to lose (or even be unaware of the loss) of nature. This is, in a sense, a modern tragedy, in that the rate of loss is speeding up. Fields we might have played in as a child are now modern housing estates, surrounding fields are cut to ribbons by new roads, everyone and everything seems crammed together. And again, we can feel this sense of 'not really comprehending what was around us' until it's no longer there! But what can be done here?

It's important that we use the recreational space surrounding us or near-by. Our connection with the land will strengthen its continued being. Quite frankly there might come times to fight for areas of beauty under threat from development. We humans might seem rulers of this earth, but nature is teeming with other forms of life. It's their earth too. We don't want to be filled with regret. Most days I spend a short amount of time signing petitions – and sometimes they really do work. It's the easiest form of effective action to protect the environment.

The song 'Big Yellow Taxi' is at times enigmatic but there is an ecological thread running through it: taking the trees and putting them in a tree museum. Or urging farmers to put away their DDT. This was an optimistic time – and there seemed the potential for unlimited change, now, as they say, WE must be the change we want. Get out in the fields (footpaths) and common land and on the heaths and mountainsides. Respect the nature you enjoy. Inform others of its wonder and complexity; its numerous flora and fauna. Encourage children to see the wonder in trees, help them listen to the birds singing and the wind rustling the willows. If we love something it will be a harder task to separate us.

I went on one of my usual walks recently and contemplated the 'loss of nature', and how with greater and greater loss would come more and more love for the nature that was left - a kind of beautiful irony perhaps – or beautiful melancholy. Many folk huddled in their homes in huddled towns and cities also need the idea, the knowledge, that there is an 'out there'. A countryside that is empty of teeming human life. Wilderness. Woods and hillsides where one can walk and where one can readjust ideas of the world – where the pace of walking forces inner reflection and calm. We MUST embrace nature. If we regret its loss, then at least we KNEW it. And will fight to keep other beautiful places – beautiful. Wordsworth wrote: *Let Nature be your teacher*!

Perhaps the final words to say regard YOU. Yourself. *Know thyself* - the adage. Knowing oneself - not coming to the end of a life and in fact never really knowing 'what you've got' or 'what you have lost'. NOW is the time to discover who and what you are. Probably miss-attributed to Mark Twain the quote: *'The two most important days in your life are the day you are born and the day you find out why'*, is a wonderful incentive to contemplate – 'WHY'!

People will inevitably enter your life, walk alongside you for a while and maybe leave. If you can embrace them for whatever time they spend with you and value – in the present – their company, then you can do no more. I am reminded here of Soren Kierkegaard's quote that: *Life can only be understood backwards; but it must be lived forwards*. It might indeed be that we can only make sense of life as we look back on it – and that is fine. But when we look back we do not want the words: *you don't know what you've got till it's gone*, resonating inside our head. We can live life forwards, understand it backwards and know that we valued all those people who touched our lives – and all the places we have experienced.

Now I have a big, yellow taxi to catch.

Chapter 9

"I smile when I'm angry
I cheat, and I lie
I do what I have to do
To get by."

- 'In my Secret life' - Leonard Cohen/Sharon Robinson

Artist: Leonard Cohen (with Sharon Robinson). Album: *Ten New Songs Year*: 2001

Do you often feel a stranger in this world? I feel estranged from this world at times – reacting to my surroundings as if I have been jilted by a lover. And this sense is exacerbated when I encounter lies and deceit, fraud and duplicity. It is very hard to be honest and open.

Sometimes people mask their emotions and smile when they are angry. They can do this for good and even practical reasons. If you force a smile it's meant to have a positive effect on your mood – tricking the mind perhaps. Or you might be feeling very angry but realise that this emotion isn't helpful and thus put on a second, smiling face. This is the mildest form of being 'two-faced'. There is also the feeling of the 'British stiff-upper lip'. Not showing emotion. This stoicism was considered a trait of the folk living on the British Isles. In many ways this is indeed the mind triumphing over the body – intention surpassing the gut emotional reactions to life.

There is also the sense that smiling when one is angry masks true intent. You know, that image of a person with a wide grin on their face, whilst behind their back they hold a knife. How do we know someone's mood? If someone can manipulate their exterior expression which contradicts their inner mood, then they can cheat us – or manipulate us. Further the lyric goes on to say, *'I cheat, and I lie'*. The lyric is about a person putting themselves first – and yes perhaps with the idea of doing whatever it takes to survive in this world.

I have always believed in HONESTY. Even as a child I was labelled 'Honest Mr. Bragg' by a company that was buying second-hand model railway equipment. My detailed description brought in a lower offer than I might have had but obviously a recognition of my honesty. I could have lied, or exaggerated, or misrepresented what I had. Those ideas didn't even come to mind. But let us look at an example at the extreme: if someone is starving (and through no real fault of their own) would it be wrong for them to steal? If someone needs to support a family and has a job interview where they lie about qualifications (but have the skills) is that wrong? Does the end justify the means?

With these examples it is a matter of looking into ourselves for the correct action. If you are starving to death and there is NO other option but to take from someone who seems to have plenty – is that immoral? Could the person who steals simply to live make an inward promise that all will be paid back in time? Would someone dying of starvation in the street make folk think and act differently – or would they simply divert round the emaciated body?

There are obviously many, many, shades of morality. I think we negotiate these nuances as we pass through life. I try not to lie or misrepresent myself, but I might lie to make someone feel better about themselves (a white lie). That is a balanced reaction. Am I doing the person a disservice by lying to them or a service? What is the overall affect? By lying to someone to make them feel better are we setting that person up for a fall? These are all nuanced reactions. Is the motivation selfishness on our part – or sensitivity to the other. When and how do we tell the truth?

Many of you, I imagine, will have friends who ask for advice or who tell you things in confidence (or otherwise), to whom you can either tell the absolute truth or you need to be 'careful'. You know them well enough to know how hurt they would be - stunned by your bluntness (as they would most likely perceive it). And what if you find out your friend (or lover) has been lying and cheating, you have seen them with a smile on their face though they in fact carried deceit or deep anger!? What if it were YOU who was being lied to or deceived?

'Do as you would be done by.' This saying that has been carried down through the centuries could well be your guidance. If the roles were reversed what would you want and expect? Of course, you are NOT that other person, you will react differently to them. But you are YOU. And you can only be you – the best and worst of you. What advice would you give to a young person you can see doing everything and anything 'to get on'?

Perhaps the crucial phrase in these lyrics is 'to get by'. 'I'm just getting by' 'I need to get by', 'Don't stop me, don't get in my way', 'Please help me.' Getting by seems like the least attractive option to pass through life – or to experience this ever-changing existence. Getting by is one step away from defeat. And it is that defeat that causes the person who is 'getting by' to behave in immoral ways. Perhaps even to USE people. This is the big worry when interacting with folk who are 'two-faced' or deceitful or fraudulent, or who lie and cheat! How do you react to them or behave with them – how can you develop a relationship, frankly, why would you WANT to develop a relationship with them? Can anyone who has told a BIG lie (or who lies repeatedly) or who has cheated (without remorse) or who does

whatever they want to get wherever they want to be –
ever be trusted?

If you are married and your partner has cheated on you
– is there any way back? Firstly, if they admit their guilt
and ask forgiveness that is different from them being
'found out'. The act is the same, but the first example
shows they have – at some level – understood their
actions. Isn't this all about understanding who and what
we are and the consequences of our thoughts and
behaviour? Imagine the pain when a trustworthy,
honest, reliable person is duped by someone they have
given their utmost trust to. A complete clash of what it
is to live a good and responsible life. The honest person
is shattered. The person who has cheated either moves
on (because they don't, in fact, care) or shows
contrition. At this point there needs to be a doubling of
trust from the honest person and an absolute NEED for
the other's honesty and baring of soul. We make
mistakes, we are tempted, we give in to the temptation
of the flesh.

You see it might give you some short-term gain to lie
and cheat, and even, for some, some long-tern gain.
But they must live with themselves. And if they CAN

live with themselves (truly?) then their moral compass is awry and should there be some form of judgement (perhaps self-judgement) at the end of this life then they will surely come to understand the consequences of their actions. Haven't we as humans – at the very LEAST – developed codes of behaviour that distinguish right from wrong? We go to war, we kill, maim, murder, cause mental and physical violence – BUT – we also have a deep sense of what is right and wrong. I think this sense cuts through cultures and even through peoples throughout history (at different levels and intensity). I'd have to think about cannibals or people who sacrificed their fellow humans to their gods, perhaps even those rearing animals in horrific conditions to be slaughtered to eat.

Let me address those who DO lie, cheat and put on a mask. By doing this, for whichever motive, you are hiding your real self, now that might be your intention - but why? If you lie what is the TRUTH that you are hiding and seemingly afraid of? If you cheat what are the SKILLS that you are lacking? Why are you afraid of your emotions? Why do you need to wear a mask to face this world? You might choose deceitful ways to get through life but is this the REAL you and the REAL life, or as the Queen lyrics go: *Is it just fantasy*? What is the point of living in a fantasy world (for more than just recreational escape) when this visceral world is so much of an experience and challenge? Or is the challenge too much? Be bold. Show yourself. Discover the true nature between the thinking you and the emotional you. As they say: you have nothing to fear but fear itself.

Get through life as YOU! To lie and cheat – to wear a false emotion makes 'getting through this life' so much cheaper. Sometimes we must hide our emotions and intent – but these are when we are under real threat of some kind. Be an example and struggle through this life with openness and honesty. Showing your true colours to the world. You can do it.

My final thoughts might seem slightly tangential - but they need saying. During our existence we lead an INTERIOR and EXTERIOR life. Not just this binary equation but there are many facets of both existences. We can be different people to different people (hence why our friends might seem so disparate) and we can be different people (to a degree) at different times in our lives, we change much of our body over time and our experiences of life will change our basic selves. Our exterior self is a perception often given by others; not outward intent. We are labelled. How EASY it is for a complicated human being to be labelled. None of us have black and white emotions - or intelligence – or behaviour, I trust the worst amongst us has some saving grace and the best amongst us carries a slightly dark shadow across their heart.

Our INTERIOR self is ours and ours alone. Elizabeth 1st did not want 'windows into men's souls'. There IS a struggle for our minds and souls but placing that carefully to one side – let us discuss OUR interior self.

The only time I think it is fine to mask or create a veneer is when we wish to preserve that inner space – our consciousness. Our thoughts are ours alone. I have thought a great deal about the nature of consciousness but for now – we can say that those thoughts we seem to 'create' or those thoughts that come seemingly 'unbidden' can be stored away inside our minds. It is NO-ONE's business what we THINK! We may wish to share our thoughts, in whichever way we desire, be it through talking/writing/painting/dancing, or we may just think about/contemplate our own thoughts! We have a rich interior life that is our REAL self. In fact, we reveal parts of ourselves to those we trust or those we think we can trust. By giving something private of ourselves to another human being we really are opening ourselves up and if they give in return then that is the beginning of a true relationship. Of course, by revealing parts of ourselves we are forever 'open'. But a true closed human being must be a very lonely creature.

Those human beings that KNOW us – or know us more than any other, are our true friends. I believe in honesty in a relationship – but even then, there are things we can, and perhaps must, hold back. Part of our strength is our autonomy. But this is about privacy and protection – we live in a world where many do, indeed, cheat and lie and smile when angry and hide behind masks and do anything they can to 'get by'. We cannot expose ourselves so much that we become everyone's puppet to manipulate at will.

It's okay to keep something back. Something that is you and you alone. If you are judged by some higher authority at the end of this life it will be a judgement of you and you alone. You are your own measurement of what is right and wrong. Stay true to yourself, 'getting by' is transient. You – you are perhaps more than a transient being. But that will be revealed – or otherwise.

I'll get by in this life by being myself and telling the truth as much as I can but keeping a sensible watch on what I reveal and to whom. We live in a world where we excrete an electronic trail for all to follow. My advice: *Be Wise*.

Chapter 10

"Love is careless in its choosing
Sweeping over cross a baby
Love descends on those defenceless
Idiot love will spark the fusion
Inspirations have I none
Just to touch the flaming dove
All I have is my love of love
And love is not loving."

-'Soul Love'- David Bowie

Artist: David Bowie. Album: *The Rise and Fall of Ziggy Stardust and the Spiders from Mars*. Year: 1972

Doves are normally thought of as a symbol of peace, but birds can represent the souls of those passed on and: In ancient Mesopotamia, doves were prominent animal symbols of Inanna-Ishtar, the goddess of love, sexuality, and war.

Why would this dove be in flames – be immolated? Why would you wish to touch it?

Okay – let's start, at the beginning!

Love is careless in its choosing. O indeed. Are there any of us who haven't experienced that capricious touch of love? Cupids encircling us and feathering down arrows. WHY do we choose a person to fall in love with and DO we choose? Is there something greater going on here? Further – is it, in fact, careless? It may be that 'love' descends upon us for all sorts of intrinsic reasons; cynically the girl reminds us of our mother/the boy reminds us of our father, we have a disposition to those with blond(e)/black/brown/grey hair, thus: are we helpless when struck by 'love'? Or do we create all the necessary backdrops to allow that love to flourish?

EXCEPT:

It takes two to tango. You can love somebody, and that person might not love you. You can do all the things one could possibly imagine to try and make that person love you – but if they haven't had the careless touch then no matter how TRUE your love seems it will not be requited. This is the sadistic little trick of love, it seeks out some to fill with un-bridled passion and then freezes the object of this desire. And sometimes two people seem to 'fall in love' (that's an interesting idea isn't it?) - to fall, helplessly in love. And what exactly IS this love? Shall I compare it to a Summer's Day?

If we fall in love with someone who does not fall in love with us, then we can (possibly) do the following:

1/ We can negate this feeling within and extricate ourselves from our desired one.

In literature it would be running off to a nunnery or working on a ship sailing to the farthest part of the world. It's not easy. It requires rationale, a rationale that seems to leave us somewhat when we have fallen – head over heels. In some way – negating our feelings seems a huge betrayal. If we fall in love how the heck can we freeze to death that emotion? If we generated this 'falling in love' it was unconscious, deep within us, out of our control. We MIGHT be able to walk away from love as a means of sacrifice, putting our desired one above ourselves, maybe becoming a nun or a sailor in a flash of near insanity (not wishing to belittle either) and thus removing ourselves physically, which would, indeed, give time to reflect on the hopelessness of our desires. Out of sight, out of mind. Let's face it – I expect many of us have 'been in love' but one of the two has gone away (to university/another country/another job elsewhere) to find that the one left out of sight has – alas – been put out of mind for yet another love. The agency of love seems capricious, tricky, has a sadistic sense of humour and a penchant for histrionics. Maybe it's all a test for something much, much deeper.

2/ We can try with all our might (intellect, humour, bravado, skills etc.) to MAKE that person love us.

Perhaps the saddest of spectacles. Pathetic in its heroic attempt. **You CAN NOT make someone love you unless they want to love you.** But sometimes perseverance DOES pay off. Your tenacity is rewarded by a change of heart. Perhaps the person you desire is awakened to see something new and wonderful in you – and the careless touch of love does indeed touch them too. Being there for someone through thick and thin can create a deeper kind of love, one that is nurtured through time. Please, do not turn into a 'stalker', you MUST remain dignified, (in the same way that at the end of a relationship it is right and noble to fight for that relationship but at some point, this nobility gives way to utter neediness). Remain dignified. Slowly, slowly, allow your rational mind to shade over the red colour of love and lust. Indeed, remaining calm and cool is perhaps the ONLY thing that could, paradoxically, bring a lover back. Indulge me here – when I was a young man I wrote these lyrics (yes, somewhat cynical):

Haven't met a girl yet who hasn't lied
Tell you her you want her... and she's gone away to hide
Tell her you don't want her and she's cried
And when you don't care she's by your side.

(If my memory serves me well – I think there's a copy of this song on a cassette tape somewhere!) Cynical enough but I DID capture the capriciousness of love.

3/ Be who we are. Behave exactly as you would normally behave – with charm and courtesy. Because if anyone falls in love with you, you want them to fall in love with YOU.

As a man I have the notion of 'being tested' of course – and this certainly has happened.

Love descends on those defenceless souls. Well yes it does, often. The feeling of love – the state of being in love is beyond our control, because control would destroy that very love. People are 'in love' to varying degrees between a pragmatic, developing friendship that morphs into a sexual relationship and then deep commitment – to two people besotted with each other acting like 'crazy fools' and not caring a jot about how the rest of the world views them. Love (and how much of this love is lust?) is the taking of a drug that renders us charming fools. As young folk it is the nearest thing to magic, as old folk (or rather love that has endured) it is the nearest thing, perhaps, to spirituality. Two people sacrificing for the other and – more importantly – for their children.

Idiot love will spark the fusion, is that the fusion of bodies? Is idiot love the extremity of love becoming lust? Desire for the body masking as a higher emotion? Two bodies fusing together, the mythical creature. Well – sex makes the world go around – as they say! Sex being – perhaps – the ultimate creative act (or potentially creative act). The fruit of sex is to bring into the world another UNIVERSE. By which I mean every mind is akin to a separate universe we all dwell within.

And now we are brought to my opening paragraph. *Inspirations have I none* [but doesn't love INSPIRE?!] *but to touch the flaming dove*. Normally speaking we see the dove as peace, perhaps as a new land, a new desire? A new resting place. But why the barrenness of inspiration? Is love all consuming – is it love that the dove represents, and this dove is consumed by the flames of desire? I am without inspiration as I grasp this flaming creature that will burn my hands (love 'gets us burnt'), my desire is greater than any pain. (And perhaps it is pain that brings us inspiration?)

Or is the dove – in fact – the SOUL of love. Does the dove personify the essence of love - flighty, landing wherever it wishes, free but caged? Singing in the morning light or at the setting sun. *All I have is my love of love*! To love love renders it dislocated from itself. Loving the desired, euphoric state and not the person, that is a kind of treason. A betrayal of what love is. Maybe that's like a drug too, just to be 'in' love, consumed by love, the highs and lows of love. The pain and suffering of love and the heights of sexual gratification. But it is not a noble love.

People have been tortured and killed for their love of God, for their love and adherence to ideas, for their defence of thoughts and actions. Men have gone to war for the love of their country. And these states of love can be as irrational as the love of another or as rational as a set of ideals. We can love the unknown. Bowie contradicts himself with these last words: And *love is not loving*. Or does he? Perhaps love is transcendental. True love. Does it exist? Surely, we FEEL it exists. When Titus Oats walked out of the tent on the ill-fated attempt of the British to be first to get to the South Pole – and with his words: *I may be some time*, Wasn't that LOVE? True, deep love. Is sacrifice the noblest act of love? Is there a difference between the nature of love between people and a transcendental love?

Love is not loving - because love is a state. It is a realm of being. All consuming. But surely rational too? Love is putting others first and yet not negating ourselves. Love travels the distance between the desire to fuse and the willingness to die for others. I remember the story of a man who – when a ferry capsized and began filling with water - created a bridge of his body so that others could get to safety. He negated the normally strongest urge of self-preservation, for whatever reason. Something took hold of him and elevated his soul. He became the act of love. This has just come into my head – of course the whole of human history is filled with the greatest stories of heroic acts of love.

And there is the love of God. For many this mystical union is also tangible. They love a sense of something greater. After all this song IS called *Soul Love*. Soul love is surely the deepest form of love. Soul. Intangible? Tangible? Where does soul and body meet? Is consciousness soul? Well these are big questions for another set of lyrics in the future perhaps. But we cannot deny the propensity in human beings to love a Godhead. And this love of a Godhead has inspired some of the greatest manifestations of culture/art that has ever been produced. Of course, some call this 'love' – delusional. Maybe all love is delusional?

When we first fall in love it seems that this is the first time we step out of childhood and into a magical realm beyond story books, beyond crushes, beyond the innocent 'love' we can feel for a girl or boy in our childhood. It is a time of super-consciousness. I can still feel the first time I held a girl's hand, and the time I felt as if I had been punched in the abdomen when she later betrayed me. Being in love is highly emotional – obviously – it is a real altered state of being. Like a drug. And therefore, some become addicted to loving being in love. Addicted to love. We know this lyric. This love is often youthful and overwhelming and can induce a state of un-equalled optimism, like we can change the world. Like we can REALLY change the world.

Perhaps this world – this 'happening' was created by and through love. A drop of love from a phial. A drop into the space of itself that grows – like love over time and all connected through time. A drop growing into an ocean. And we are drops of this ocean too. Two drops fusing in love. Part of a huge soul – perhaps, Fusing with God – perhaps?

Love tests itself through time. Mature love is its most sublime form. Soul love.

Chapter 11

"In the morning, I'm at work on time

My boss, he tells me

That I'm doing fine

When I'm going home

Whiskey bottle

Movie on TV

Memories make me cry

And I'm alone

Just me

Just me

Questioningly."

-'Questioningly' – Ramones

Artist: Ramones. Album: *Road to Ruin* Year 1978

Conscientious soul, at work on time. Day in day out, month in month out, year in – well you get the drift. The Boss is happy – but probably no rise! This is a side of life, he can keep in order, work routine. Routines keep many folk sane. Routines give purpose. And they lock you in. But of course, you have a mortgage to pay or rent to handover each month. Routines keep you secure. Routines pay the bills – all work and no play makes Jack a dull chap.

On his way back from work he stops off to buy a bottle of whiskey, whiskey makes you forget. Well, I must admit here that I don't like whiskey (or any spirit) and thus don't drink any. But in the past, I have drunk my share at times, well, I remember having too much Southern Comfort and returning home with a friend making – I imagine - a spectacle of ourselves. I'm not really a fan of alcohol. Some wine with a meal occasionally, some beer for its taste, but if someone is coming home from work and needs to buy whiskey 'to get through' 'to get by' (recalling previous lyrics) then that's not going to end well.

There are all sorts of arguments for and against alcohol, and I'm not going to judge – but persistent use will have its effects. Psychologically if you are using alcohol as a prop to your life, if it dulls your mind enough to continue the path you are on (which you don't want to be) then everything, every problem, every regret, will be exacerbated. This is just the way alcohol works. A quick and easy – and LEGAL fix. Without moralising – I would only say do whatever you can to cut back on what you drink. Wine with a meal – fine. Some social drinking – fine. YOU know when you're abusing it. And if you are you're going to have to decide to stop for yourself. You're going to have to change your social life and maybe even friends. Make the decision first and then stick to it. But if you DO relapse don't use that as a reason not to go back on the wagon. I don't wish to be a hypocrite here and I must only give advice that I can back up from experience, but ANY excess needs pruning: alcohol or 'recreational drugs'. Some things make you view life with greater clarity, some things make you think you're viewing life with greater clarity and some things slowly blind you.

I have lived with people who have smoked marijuana continuously, I know folk who 'can't get by' (yes, they can) without alcohol. But to straighten out your life you must get straight!

So, with the whiskey bottle by his side and with a film on the TV he has the perfect excuse not to engage with reality. And then we get to find out – a little – about his situation. I say 'he' because this feels like a he to me, but if you 'see' a female or if you ARE female then this can be applied equally. *'Memories make me cry and I am all alone.'* Memories make me cry, memories make me cry too, or maybe an inward smile – depending. Some memories are incredibly painful and their effect as visceral (almost) as the day of the reality that spawned them. What do we do about painful memories?

We seem to create thoughts constantly, they come unbidden and other thoughts (that we store) are embedded in us through time because of the power of that memory. A thought and its associate memory (re-membering) has no concrete existence. You cannot tangibly hold a thought. Interestingly this thought re-membered from the 'past' is, in fact, always carried in the 'present'. Though of course a 'new' thought can have more power than an 'old' thought (memory) and vice versa. Because the thought can be held again in the present (or is always there but accessed in the present) it affects us in a similar fashion. We remember a BAD time and it is as if that badness comes back to us. Haunts our mind. This ghost can chase away the other thoughts with its power. It can sit above all with a brooding, malevolent presence, it can chase away any good thoughts or optimistic thoughts. It is powerful!

The thought needs to be dislodged. Or exhausted by its constant presence. The memory of things 'passed' needs to be held in place, in a thought-cell (if you will); it may/may not fade with time. But if you can hold it in its cell and oversee it when you let it out (or rather when it escapes) – capturing it and interrogating it, you can, slowly, diminish its power. Yes, alcohol will take away these thoughts (or their power) in the short-term (or long-term abuse) but then you are always at the mercy of either spirit - the ghost of the memory or the whiskey etc. Perhaps the best action is to look upon this painful memory as an 'outsider'. This you CAN do with a thought – because we are not 're-thinking' the thought as such (but re-membering) we can, therefore, observe. We cannot think ourselves back into our bodies at the time of the original thought, but we do feel the sensations and re-live the experience again as if a 'third-party'. So, you must become the observer of your past.

As the observer you are partially immune. You can feel sympathy, empathy for the memory of you or your response to the memory BUT – you are now removed from that. You have moved on – mentally and physically. That is a natural, organic change. You will NEVER be the person who had that bad memory. You can't be. You are linked but you are now objective. Look at yourself. Look down on yourself (as if from above). Try and hold that memory and watch it slip slidin' away, like trying to remember a face from many years ago – you seem to see it askance. The power of the memory is only what you allow. This is also fact. Of course, we are a sum of all our experiences. Sometimes we are flooded by bad experiences, a torrent, a current seemingly washing us away. We need to grab hold of a rock or a tree-trunk or someone's hand. We can do this!

We need to live in the (seeming) present too. Living NOW, being active, having goals, being productive – dare I say it – being CREATIVE! These will help chase away these demons. Walking works too, you become locked into the natural pace of your walking rhythm (as I have already described). Because you cannot go faster than your walk you are forced into an awareness of your surroundings and a natural reflection seems to take place, by taking yourself OUTSIDE of the rush you become absorbed in this slowed down, almost meditative state. You will find yourself able to comprehend your problems, thoughts will come to you un-bidden and be surprisingly helpful. Walking eases the mind, puts things into perspective, you don't need to go far but just far enough to become inside yourself. Once you've gone a certain distance you just must continue, or return, by yielding to this, the mind can relax. Really. It's surprising (unless of course you already practice this). It's as if the active conscious mind is put to one side. There are other ways to get to this state too – I can do this by drumming (the rhythms taking over) or by playing the flute (here helped by the need to have controlled breathing). In all these actions the busy, busy, pre-occupied conscious mind and rushing thoughts are calmed. Things begin to make sense. Twenty minutes a day. Or – if you can't walk, get a cheap acoustic guitar. Don't have high expectations – but strumming between two chords (this will take a few weeks) on a TUNED guitar will have the same absorbing yet freeing sense. It will also give a sense of direction. And if none of this is possible or desirable then sit down with a pen and paper or at your keyboard with a new document opening on the screen and WRITE! Anything! Whatever comes into your head. Maybe even write about that bad memory, because if you DO it will be like inching off that white sheet of the ghost. I have advised these actions previously – they CAN work for you. Once the ghost is exposed it will become NOTHING without its white sheet.

Some people I know have swapped a bad addiction for a healthy one. Perhaps recognising they have an addictive impulse the destructive addiction has been supplanted. Having a regular routine (addiction?) for physical exercise will create the space and time to concentrate on the body's health and with that mental health too. If this new 'addiction' is completely healthy it can turn around the effects of previous drug/alcohol misuse. If you couple this with an 'addiction' to eating healthy food, then the body AND mind can repair and heal themselves. It's never too late. It might take being at rock bottom before the decision to change is made – but I DO know folk that have done exactly that. Making that decision is brave, sticking to it shows courage and tenacity. The very same impulses that feed a bad addiction can be used to feed a good 'addiction'. Of course, anything can go 'too far' – but if someone has stopped themselves on a fatal downward spiral that shows they have some fundamental strength which can always be drawn on. Please acknowledge that if you have turned your life around – and never forget it! You are stronger than you think. Don't be afraid to ask for help either, sometimes you'll be surprised at the help you can and do get.

I'm alone. I'm alone.

Well we are ALL alone. Even in the greatest of throngs in a teeming city – we are alone. John Donne wrote: *No man is an island*. By which he meant that we are all connected in some fashion (there are also his famous lines: *And therefore, never send to know for whom the bell tolls; it tolls for thee*). We're all in it together – and there is help and hindrance all around us – but nevertheless, we as individuals, have sovereignty – only WE can know the extent of our mind. The mind in which we dwell.

There are many folk who thrive being alone, who seem self-sufficient. They are at ease with their solitude and peace. Others seem to be running away from themselves and crave company always. This is the crux, if we are alone and suffering then being alone magnifies the pain. It takes a very strong person to go through hard times alone and stay firm. A weaker person or a person ill at ease with their thoughts and mental pain are going to find being alone so much harder. But equally if they have deep mental problems, then going out all the time, or drinking alcohol all the time, or taking drugs all the time, won't help. There must be a balance of quiet reflection and moral support.

Fortunately, in these modern days many people have access to a computer and the internet and can gain knowledge and community via the computer screen. It is a kind of 'virtual' help but then thoughts are 'virtual' too aren't they? And it's our thoughts that need helping and/or changing or improving. We can be open to others too and at least let folk know that we WILL listen to them, and we WILL open our homes to them. And we can develop empathy.

Of course, there are also memories that make us cry but not in a wholly bad way. Is it bad to remember lost loved ones and shed a tear, or even to recall our childhood (or the childhood of our children) and shed a tear for this lost youth, innocence? We can cry over memories and it can be very therapeutic. And after crying we can also have a wide smile on our face as we recall the person we have loved – that we still love. They are still part of us – after all.

Music can take us back to a time and a place with the speed of an arrow hitting a target. Music can transport us to another existence. And we can draw a lot of support and help from the lyrics of songs that have been with us from that very first listen. Songwriters have interpreted all the vast range of human experience, often of sorrow and yearning. When I feel sad then listening to a sad song helps me feel better. Music can reflect the state we are in and resonate with that feeling so much that it seems to shake it off. Music is the great healer. We are never alone when we have music.

Have belief in yourself. You made it this far. You made it from being a help-less baby passed from arm to arm. You made it through school (or even 'bunking off'). All the setbacks in your life haven't stopped you from being you. The heartaches have made you a better person, haven't they? Even if you're suffering debt and there seems no way out, there always IS. If you trust yourself and those around you. If you're lying in the street and a thousand people walk around and past you there is always one who will stop and help and give you some kindness. Humans can seem a bad lot at times but it's also in our nature to help others, even if we seem hardened by the cruelties of life, so many will still find the time and energy to give a helping hand to those less fortunate.

We are all heading for the same 'place' of course. That's sobering enough. I think TS Eliot said (or is oft cited as saying): *It's the journey not the arrival that matters.* He certainly wrote: *We shall not cease from exploration, and the end of all our exploring will be to arrive where we started and know the place for the first time.*

Can you imagine our existence on this planet without music or without the great insights of wordsmiths? Take time out from your busy lives and maybe take a fragment of lyric or poetry or lyrical poetry (indeed!) and contemplate and reflect on the words. Let them speak to you. Write your own! Listen to what you have to say to yourself.

Extend your horizons and if you can't travel in reality then travel in your mind. This world and your place in it, is your making.

Good luck on your journey.

Chapter 12

"And I can feel the stars getting closer
And I can feel you by my side
And I can feel an arm wrap around me
Yes I can feel you by my side
Don't look back 'cus it's coming
Don't look here 'cus it's gone
And when you least expect it will fall upon your
shoulder
Sometimes stand still – better not run."

-'Some Answers' – Tim Bragg

Artist: Tim Bragg Album: *Revamped 3 & Been Before*
Year: 2014/2018

Should I apologise for including my lyrics with the greats? Perhaps. But it's not often – I presume – that a writer is drawn back to his own lyrics to guide his life. And there is something about these lyrics that DOES draw me back. And for this reason, I want to share my objective thoughts on what they might say and have to offer.

Surely, I know what my lyrics say? Yes and no! I knew what they said at some point – but as with any writing their meaning opens as they become public. Interpretation is the key and we interpret things differently at various times in our life. And now after a few years these lyrics come to me at times. There is also the sense that lyrics and songs come to us from a 'different place'. How much control do we have over that. All of you can try this: sit down with a pen and some paper. And without THINKING – just write. Let the pen take over from your conscious mind. See what happens.

I can feel the stars getting closer, I can feel heaven getting closer maybe, or God (or The Great Creator of the Great Happening). And I can feel this mystical presence near me. I am comforted by the wrapping round of an arm. This could also refer to a deceased friend or relative giving comfort from beyond this life. That feeling of some presence that warms and reassures. And yes – I can feel that person by my side.

How often do we have this feeling of reassurance and support? I think we can all take strength and hope from these fleeting moments, in a car, driving home, or from a gig, or to see a friend. At night. And then the sudden sense of NOT being alone. And at this moment there is a presence by your side.

Don't look back – [because] *it's coming.* What's coming? Something good or bad? The past? Don't look back to the past because it's coming TO you, it's on the way. Have faith – if you will. Then*: don't look here – cause it's gone*! It isn't HERE. Where is it? And yet if you stand still it will be with you. The idea here is that you can chase butterflies, but you may never grasp them – you may kill them by grasping them. But if you stand still a butterfly may perch on your shoulder, on your nose even – be there right in front of your face. Alighting upon you.

Are you always running after a dream? Can you see the wood but not the trees? Are you always pursuing something that will come to you if you just *'let it be'*? Let's apply some of these ideas to our lives. There can be something noble in the pursuit of things, courageous even, and yet there is also pathos in the struggle.

Sometimes – perhaps when you need something the most it is better to stand still, firm. Stand boldly. It is coming and will come to you. Don't run, don't hide don't search in a panicked state. Be still. And then – when you least expect it - it will fall gently upon your shoulder – like that elusive butterfly.

These words speak to me about calmness and the inner-knowledge that everything will eventually come that needs to come to you. This idea ties in with a lot of the lyrics we have looked at. You can't always get what you want, but what you need. The nearer your destination the more you're slip slidin' away. Do we try too hard? How do we find that balance between inertia and hysterical action? Are we talking about fate here and, indeed, is there such a thing as fate? Should we resign ourselves to higher powers and wait for something to happen!? Well perhaps not.

Life is a balance between what IS, what might have been and what could be. Are we at the mercy of fate or are we the creators of our own lives/destinies? Of course, there are many ideas about this and these questions are as old as human beings. There's some interesting modern scientific ideas about fate and freewill. Do we live in the perpetual 'present'; do we linger a few seconds behind this 'present' in a past that persuades us we ARE in the present? Does our conscious mind trick us? Well – whichever of these is true we seem to live in the 'here and now' and we seem to direct our will (again some scientific research suggests our 'decisions' lag the physical action!). At this point we must look at how life appears to respond to us and our desires.

It may well be that life is – to an extent – mapped out. This could be for a myriad of reasons, mostly beyond our control. But empirical evidence would suggest we can will certain action. We can force ourselves off the well-trodden track, we can force ourselves off OR ONTO the 'straight and narrow' path. We CAN decide at a deep level to change course. Now if this is a trick by our consciousness so be it – the experience is equally valid. Rather than play the role of a puppet or sink into nihilistic gloom and despair and inertia we can choose to snap out of a nightmare, or we can wait optimistically for something to guide us, or we can make that internal decision that we will, we want, and we can - change! THEN when we least expect it to happen, when we're not falling over ourselves to grasp the butterfly, it will settle upon us. Now this doesn't mean – as stated – that doing nothing is the answer. Doing nothing will keep those butterflies well beyond arm's length. We must find a course between desperate struggle and grasping and crushing these beautiful creatures and hiding ourselves away in a darkened, lifeless room. By which I mean taking decisions to behave in a certain fashion and having the will to do so! This will bring that arm around our shoulder, helping and guiding us on our way.

It can be a spark, a word, a sentence, something we see or hear, a person coming into our lives that is the change falling on our shoulders. Seemingly from nowhere but propelled from the 'future' by our innermost needs. We have drawn this change to us. We haven't driven it away by frantic desperation; we haven't killed possibility by the twins: aggression and neediness, we have decided to be something greater. And at the moment of this conception we have drawn in the possibilities of real hope and change. At our lowest moment, deep in depression, none of us is exempt from help and guidance. None.

In a sense you might argue that I'm talking about 'faith'. This faith being a belief in our role on this earth. Maybe we can think of it like this:

Think of a huge, detailed map. We have the town of our birth and the town of our death. In-between the two are multiple, near infinite routes we can take. Perhaps our DNA, our infancy, our schooling, either open new roads or close off possible directions. Our predispositions give us a general direction and a personalised map. We could sit back and let life take us on a ride – but that way might lead us through fertile valleys or into swamps and fast-raging river torrents. So, at every crossways when we don't know what to do and when darkness begins to descend on us we need to keep our self-faith.

It's no good rushing down a direction where we cannot see beyond a few feet. No good sitting down and giving up because we can't decide - and all ways seem to pose threat. We need to stop, think and trust ourselves. At this point with the stars twinkling about us a helping hand may well indeed come – passing us a torch (light at the end of the tunnel). We can shine it on the map – using our own volition and see the best route to continue (always limited of course as many crossroads will fall on our path). We can smile inwardly and thank that comforting help that rested on our shoulders. We trusted that a way would be shown, and it was.

This is all about trust. Trust and faith. If help and faith are encapsulated by a butterfly we must accept the butterfly's beauty and fragility. You cannot compel such a creature, but in your being still and confident it will flutter upon you. Resting lightly. We know that many lives are lead that end in, or experience, tragedy – we understand this. And I cannot speak for all those lives, but I believe there is something beyond us. Beyond our mortal understanding. Our lives here on earth are self-created: we see, hear, touch, feel and speak, think in our brain, in our mind, in our thoughts. We live within our thoughts. We CAN alter our perceptions and actions through concentrated thought. We can – at the very least – allow help to manifest. *Sometimes stand still – better not run*.

Collect your thoughts. Look at the world and your place in it. Think about those people or circumstances that have come into your life and have seemed to push you along. Maybe words from a book you have read. Maybe a song you have heard. Maybe even the lyrics you have read. We all need help from time to time. With these lyrics I am arguing for the quiet help that flutters into your life, for the sense of the presence of those we love being with us and helping in dark times, or lonely times, or times when we despair. Go inward. Close your eyes and feel the blackness of your inner-self. See the stars in your own Heaven. Feel the sense of someone or something close to you giving you comfort. Let faith in yourself come with each breath, trust in yourself and your being on this earth. Take the torch that is offered and illuminate the map and where you find yourself.

The song I wrote is called *'Some Answers'*. I am no different from you in that I am also searching for answers. And there are times when I feel at an utter loss. But I have never been abandoned in this life. And nor shall you.

Songs

Slip Slidin' Away is a 1977 song written and recorded by Paul Simon, from his compilation album *Greatest Hits, Etc.*

Label: Columbia

Publisher: Universal Music Group

You Can't Always Get What You Want is a song by the Rolling Stones on their 1969 album *Let It Bleed*. Written by Mick Jagger and Keith Richards.

(From Wikipedia: The song was originally released on the B-side of *"Honky Tonk Women"* in July 1969. Although it did not chart at the time, London Records re-serviced the single in 1973 and *"You Can't Always Get What You Want"* reached number 42 on the *Billboard Hot 100* and number 34 on the *CashboxTop 100* Singles chart. One of the Stones' most popular recordings, it has since appeared on the compilations

Hot Rocks, Singles Collection (single version), *Forty Licks, Rolled Gold+: The Very Best of the Rolling Stones* (2007 edition), *Singles 1968-1971*(single version*), Slow Rollers* (single version) and *GRRR!* (single version).) Label: Decca (UK) London (US)

Hey Jude, was released in August 1968 as the first single from the Beatles' record label Apple Records. *Hey Jude,* was the A-side, the B-side being *Revolution.* Released: 26 August 1968. Format: 7-inch vinyl. Recorded: 31 July – 1 August 1968, Trident Studios, London. Genre: Rock/Pop. Length: 7:11

Songwriter(s): Lennon–McCartney

Producer(s): George Martin, The Beatles.

Publisher: Northern Songs Ltd.

Label: Apple

(Singles chronology: *Lady Madonna* (1968) *Hey Jude* (1968) *Get Back* (1969).)

Stairway to Heaven by Led Zeppelin – a US promotional single. From the untitled fourth album known as: *Led Zeppelin IV* Released: 8th November 1971 Recorded:

1971 Studio: Island, London. Genre: Progressive rock/ folk rock/ hard rock Length: 8:02

Songwriter(s): Jimmy Page/Robert Plant Producer(s): Jimmy Page

Label: Atlantic

Publisher: Superhype Publ. Inc.

Masters of War is a song by Bob Dylan, written over the winter of 1962–63 and released on the album The *Freewheelin' Bob Dylan* in the spring of 1963.

Burning Heart is a song by Survivor and was sung by Jimi Jamison. It appeared in the film *Rocky IV* (1985) and on the soundtrack album. The song reached number 2 on the *Billboard Hot 100* chart. The song seems to have been inspired by the Cold War. *Burning Heart* appeared in the 2013 video game *Grand Theft Auto V* and an episode of the television series *Psych*.

Writers: Jim Peterik and Frankie Sullivan

Label: Scotti Bros.

Wicked Game is a song by American rock musician Chris Isaak, released from his third studio album *Heart Shaped World* (1989). Despite being released as a single in 1990, it did not become a hit until it was later featured in the David Lynch film +(1990). Lee Chesnut, an Atlanta radio station music director who loved David Lynch films, began playing the song and it quickly became a nationwide top ten hit in January 1991, reaching number 6 on the *Billboard Hot 100* chart, making it the first hit song of his career. (The above is taken from Wikipedia.)

Label: Reprise

Publisher: C Isaak Music Pub. Comp.

Big Yellow Taxi is a song written, composed, and originally recorded by Canadian singer-songwriter Joni Mitchell in 1970, and originally released on her album *Ladies of the Canyon*.

Label: Reprise

Publisher: Crazy Crow Music

In My Secret Life is a song written and performed by Leonard Cohen and Sharon Robinson. Bob Metzger plays the guitar. The song first appears on the album *Ten New Songs*, released in 2001.

Label: Columbia

Publisher: Sharon Robinson Songs

Soul Love is a song written by David Bowie and recorded on 12 November 1971 that appeared as the second track on his album *The Rise and Fall of Ziggy Stardust and the Spiders from Mars* (1972).

 Label: RCA Victor (original release)

Publisher: Chrysalis Songs (BMI)

(Digital Remaster ℗ 1999. The copyright in this sound recording is owned by Jones/Tintoretto Entertainment Co., LLC. under exclusive license to EMI Records Ltd. © 1999 Jones/Tintoretto Entertainment Co., LLC.)

Questioningly was on *Road to Ruin*: the fourth studio album by American punk rock band the Ramones, released on September 21, 1978

Label: Sire Records

Publishers: Blue Disque Music Co Inc. /Mutated Music/Taco Tunes Inc./W B Music Corp.

Some Answers is a song written by Tim Bragg from the album *Revamped 3* (2014) which includes the award-winning song *Infinity*. *Some Answers* will also be appearing on the album *Been Before* to be released later in 2018.

Label: CDBaby

Printed in Great Britain
by Amazon